A Pelican Original

A Seventh Man

John Berger was born in London in 1926. He attended both the Central and the Chelsea Schools of Art and started his working life as a painter. His published works include a book of essays called ' Permanent Red' (1960); ' Success and Failure of Picasso' (1965); four novels: ' A Painter of Our Time' (1958), ' The Foot of Clive' (1962), ' Corker's Freedom' (1964) and ' G.' (1972); and 'Art and Revolution' (1969). He writes regularly for 'New Society'. He has also written ' A Fortunate Man' with Jean Mohr (1967).

Jean Mohr was born in Geneva in 1925 and obtained a diploma in commercial science at the University of Geneva. After a year in publicity he worked for the International Red Cross in Palestine and Jordan, then went to Paris as a painter. Since 1954 he has worked professionally as a photographer in Geneva, contributing to many magazines, doing assignments for the World Health Organization and International Labour Office, and contributing to the Recontres series, 'Atlas des voyages'.

Sven Blomberg was born in Helsinki in 1920. He studied economics in Antwerp, then worked as a painter first in England and since 1946 in France. He collaborated on ' Ways of Seeing' (Penguin Books, 1972).

By the same author:

A Painter of Our Time
Success and Failure of Picasso
Corker's Freedom
A Fortunate Man
Art and Revolution
Selected Essays
G.
Ways of Seeing

A SEVENTH MAN

A book of images and words
about the experience of
Migrant Workers in Europe

John Berger   Jean Mohr

with the collaboration of
Sven Blomberg

Penguin Books

Penguin Books Ltd,
Harmondsworth, Middlesex, England
Penguin Books Inc.,
7110 Ambassador Road, Baltimore, Maryland 21207, U.S.A.
Penguin Books Australia Ltd,
Ringwood, Victoria, Australia
Penguin Books Canada Ltd,
41 Steelcase Road West, Markham, Ontario, Canada
Penguin Books (N.Z.) Ltd,
182–190 Wairau Road, Auckland 10, New Zealand

First published 1975

Copyright © John Berger, text; Jean Mohr, pictures; 1975

Made and printed in Great Britain by
Hazell Watson & Viney Ltd, Aylesbury, Bucks
Set in Monotype Clarendon

This book
was made by:

Sven Blomberg, painter
Richard Hollis, designer
Jean Mohr, photographer
John Berger, writer

A Note to the Reader

This book concerns a dream / nightmare. By what right can we call the lived experience of others a dream / nightmare? Not because the facts are so oppressive that they can weakly be termed nightmarish; nor because hopes can weakly be termed dreams.

In a dream the dreamer wills, acts, reacts, speaks, and yet submits to the unfolding of a story which he scarcely influences. The dream happens to him. Afterwards he may ask another to interpret it. But sometimes a dreamer tries to break his dream by deliberately waking himself up. This book represents such an intention within a dream which the subject of the book and each of us is dreaming.

To outline the experience of the migrant worker and to relate this to what surrounds him – both physically and historically – is to grasp more surely the political reality of the world at this moment. The subject is European, its meaning is global. Its theme is unfreedom. This unfreedom can only be fully recognized if an objective economic system is related to the subjective experience of those trapped within it. Indeed, finally, the unfreedom is that relationship.

The book consists of images and words. Both should be read in their own terms. Only occasionally is an image used to illustrate the text. The photographs, taken over a period of years by Jean Mohr, say things which are beyond the reach of words. The pictures in sequence make a statement: a statement which is equal and comparable to, but different from, that of the text. When documentary information makes it easier to look into a picture, the picture has a caption beside it. When such information is not immediately necessary on the page, the caption can be found in the list of illustrations at the end of the book. A few photographs were taken, not by Jean Mohr, but by Sven Blomberg, who also contributed much to the design and visual structure of the book.

In the text there are a dozen quotations which are acknowledged at the end, but not on the pages on which they are printed. They relate to facts and processes whose implications are larger than those of authorship.

Many migrant workers in north-western Europe come from former colonial territories – West Indians, Pakistanis and Indians in Britain, Algerians in France, workers from Surinam in Holland, etc. Their working and living conditions are often similar to those of migrants who come from southern Europe. They experience the same exploitation. But the history of their presence in the metropolitan centres belongs to the history of colonialism and neo-colonialism. In order to define as sharply as possible the new phenomenon of millions of peasants migrating to countries with which they have had no previous connection, we have concentrated here on the migrants who come from Europe. This is also why neither images nor text refer directly to Britain, where the majority of immigrants come from former colonies. The distinction is an artificial one, but it makes for a clearer focus.

Among the migrant workers in Europe there are probably two million women. Some work in factories; many work in domestic service. To write of their experience adequately would require a book in itself. We hope this will be done. Ours is limited to the experience of the male migrant worker.

The book was written in 1973 and the first half of 1974. Since then capitalism has faced its worst economic crisis since the Second World War. This crisis has led to the cutting back of production and unemployment. The number of migrant workers in some sectors has been reduced. A few of the statistics given in the text may therefore be out of date. Yet Western Europe's continued dependence on millions of migrant workers, even during such a crisis, shows that the economic system can no longer exist without migrant labour.

1. DEPARTURE

The Seventh

If you set out in this world,
better be born seven times.
Once, in a house on fire,
once, in a freezing flood,
once, in a wild madhouse,
once, in a field of ripe wheat,
once, in an empty cloister,
and once among pigs in a sty.
Six babes crying, not enough:
you yourself must be the seventh.

When you must fight to survive,
let your enemy see seven.
One, away from work on Sunday,
one, starting his work on Monday,
one, who teaches without payment,
one, who learned to swim by drowning,
one, who is the seed of a forest,
and one, whom wild forefathers protect,
but all their tricks are not enough:
you yourself must be the seventh.

If you want to find a woman,
let seven men go for her.
One, who gives his heart for words,
one, who takes care of himself,

one, who claims to be a dreamer,
one, who through her skirt can feel her,
one, who knows the hooks and snaps,
one, who steps upon her scarf:
let them buzz like flies around her.
You yourself must be the seventh.

If you write and can afford it,
let seven men write your poem.
One, who builds a marble village,
one, who was born in his sleep,
one, who charts the sky and knows it,
one, whom words call by his name,
one, who perfected his soul,
one, who dissects living rats.
Two are brave and four are wise;
you yourself must be the seventh.

And if all went as was written,
you will die for seven men.
One, who is rocked and suckled,
one, who grabs a hard young breast,
one, who throws down empty dishes,
one, who helps the poor to win,
one, who works till he goes to pieces,
one, who just stares at the moon.
The world will be your tombstone:
you yourself must be the seventh.

Attila József

In Germany (and in Britain) one out of seven manual
workers is an immigrant. In France, Switzerland and Belgium
about 25 per cent of the industrial labour force are foreigners.

A friend came to see me in a dream. From far away.
And I asked in the dream: 'Did you come by photograph or train?'
All photographs are a form of transport and an expression of
absence.

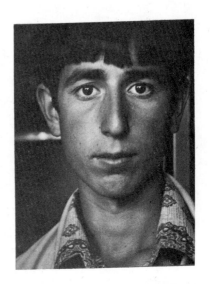

He. The existence of a migrant worker.

He looks for the photo among the over-handled papers,
stuffed in his jacket. He finds it. In handing it over, he imprints
his thumb on it. Almost deliberately, as a gesture of possession. A
woman or perhaps a child. The photo defines an absence. Even if it
is ten years old it makes no difference. It holds open, preserves the
empty space which the sitter's presence will, hopefully, one day fill
again. He puts it immediately back in his pocket without glancing
at it. As if there were a need for it in his pocket.

The photographs in this book work in the opposite way.

A photograph of a boy in the rain, a boy unknown to you or me. Seen in the dark-room when making the print, or seen in this book when reading it, the image conjures up the vivid presence of the unknown boy. To his father it would define the boy's absence.

In north-western Europe, excluding Britain, there are approximately eleven million migrant workers. The exact number is impossible to estimate because a probable two million are living and working without proper papers, illegally. A United Nations survey has estimated that by 1980 there will be half as many again.

17

The American business magazine, ' Fortune ', states unequivocally that migrant workers 'now appear indispensable to Europe's economy. What was initially a temporary expedient has become something close to a permanent necessity.'

Apart from a loft, there is one room in the house: a large one with an uneven earth floor. The door opens on to a yard of the same earth: a boy of ten, the eldest in the family, has dug a hole in which to make charcoal. When the branches of wood are burning in the hole he covers them over with earth, smothering them, so that they burn exceedingly slowly. The air is cold and the boy's hands and ears are red. A little smoke comes out of the earth mysteriously.

The father is in the forest felling and cutting. After midnight, having loaded the wood on to a mule, he will leave on his seven-hour journey to the nearest market village where, with a hundred or so other peasants from the high plateau, he will hope to sell the wood. (For stakes, fences, buildings: not for burning.) The night will be frosty but there is a moon. Occasionally a hoof will strike a spark from the road. He will return the following night, having hopefully sold the wood.

In a hollow of earth near the centre of the room another small wood fire is burning and in the fire are two large flat stones. On the tops of these stones the mother is baking bread. The bread is thin and unleavened. It never really bakes and remains heavy and damp. She makes the bread twice a day and it is the staple of the family diet. In the room, apart from the mother, there is a grandmother, three younger children, a baby and an ox. The animal's ribs are very pronounced, and its hide has the dead cloth-like look that comes from being under-fed. On the ground near the ox, because it is warmer there with the straw and mulch, is a wooden cradle in which the baby, tightly swaddled, sleeps. (Neither the story of the stable in Bethlehem, nor the fact that the cradle is hand-painted with flowers like one in a museum, redeem this scene.) Except for the cradle and two small milking stools, there is no other furniture. But in the corner of the room farthest from the door there is a very large wooden platform, the height of a table, on which are strewn rags and old clothes. This is the bed where all the family sleep. The main difference in the winter between waking and sleeping is the cold. It is warmer sleeping under the rags and on the top of the sheep; on the side of the wooden platform are two planks that lift up to make an entrance; every evening the seven family sheep rush into the pen under the bed. When the father returns, there will be seven bodies on the bed and seven sheep underneath.

In current descriptions of the world, the major industrial societies are often described as 'metropolitan'. At first glance this can be taken as a simple description of their internal development, in which the metropolitan cities have become dominant. But when we look at it more closely, in its real historical development, we find that what is meant is an extension to the whole world of that division of functions which in the nineteenth century was a division of functions within a single state. The 'metropolitan' societies of Western Europe and North America are the 'advanced', 'developed', industrialized states; centres of economic, political and cultural power. In sharp contrast with them, though there are many intermediate stages, are other societies which are seen as 'underdeveloped': still mainly agricultural or 'under-industrialized'. The 'metropolitan' states, through a system of trade, but also through a complex of economic and political controls, draw food and, more critically, raw materials from these areas of supply, this effective hinterland, that is also the greater part of the earth's surface and that contains the great majority of its people.

Every Sunday we children would play outside the church before going to mass, and we'd say to each other: 'After mass, let's go to the cross at the entrance to the village and from there see if we can make a hole and get up to heaven . . .'

Migrant workers come from underdeveloped economies. The term 'underdeveloped' has caused diplomatic embarrassment. The word 'developing' has been substituted. 'Developing' as distinct from 'developed'. The only serious contribution to this semantic discussion has been made by the Cubans, who have pointed out that there should be a transitive verb: to underdevelop. An economy is underdeveloped because of what is being done around it, within it and to it. There are agencies which underdevelop.

21

Every day he hears about the metropolis. The name of the city changes. It is all cities, overlaying one another and becoming a city that exists nowhere but which continually transmits promises. These promises are not transmitted by any single means. They are implicit in the accounts of those who have already been to a city. They are transmitted by machinery, by cars, tractors, tin-openers, electric drills, saws. By ready-made clothes. By the planes which fly across the sky. By the nearest main road. By tourist coaches. By a wrist watch. They are there on the radio. In the news. In the music. In the manufacture of the radio itself. Only by going to this city can the meaning of all the promises be realized. They have in common a quality of openness.

The road leads out of the village, across the plain or through hills. After a few kilometres the village is out of sight; the sky continues over the land. He is far more aware of the phenomenon of the horizon than most city dwellers. Yet it is openness that the metropolis represents for him. Within that openness is opportunity. The opportunity to earn a living; to have enough money to act.

The inhabitant of the modern metropolis tends to believe that it is always somehow possible to scrape a bare living off the land – unless it is a desert: or a dust bowl. The belief is part of the Romantic idealization of Nature, encouraged by the fact that the city lives off a surplus transported from the country-side and amassed in the city where it suggests the wealth of a cornucopia. The belief is far – in every sense – from the truth. Nature has to be bribed to yield enough. Peasants everywhere know this. Rural poverty means that there is nothing to bribe with. It is not a question of working harder. The further working of the land is withdrawn as a possibility.

24

FAMILY LIVING IN A CAVE, ANDALUSIA

SWEDISH COUNTRY CHILDREN, 1913

25

According to the capitalist ethic, poverty is a state from which an individual or a society is delivered by enterprise. Enterprise is judged by the criterion of Productivity as a value in itself. Hence underdevelopment as a condition of locked, inescapable poverty is inconceivable to capitalism. Yet capitalism holds nearly half the world in that condition. This contradiction between theory and practice is one of the reasons why capitalism and its cultural institutions can no longer explain either itself or the world.

Modern rural poverty has a social rather than a natural basis. The land becomes barren through lack of irrigation or seed or fertilizers or equipment. The unproductivity of the land then leads to unemployment or underemployment. For example: an able-bodied man may be forced to spend his whole day grazing two cattle. The social basis of this poverty, however, is disguised. The economic relations which intervene between the land and the peasants – the share-cropping system, the system of land tenure, the money-lending system, the marketing system – come to be seen as part of the barrenness of the land, part of the incontestable truth that you can't make bread from stone.

Those who have left and succeeded in the city and come
back, are heroes. He has talked with them. They take him aside
as though inviting him into their conspiracy. They hint that there
are secrets which can only be divulged and discussed with those
who have also been there. One such secret concerns women. (They
show him photographs in colour of naked women but they will
not say who they are.) Another concerns certain men who must
never be insulted or crossed. Another is about how long it takes to
walk out of the city. Another is about the buildings into which it is
absolutely forbidden to enter. What is not a secret at all are the
wages, the things to be bought, the amount that can be saved, the
variety of cars, the way women dress, what there is to eat and
drink, the hours worked, the arguments won, the cunning which is
needed on all occasions. He recognizes that they are boasting when
they talk. But he accords them the right to boast, for they have
returned with money and presents which are proof of their
achievement. Some drove back in their own cars.

Whilst listening, he visualizes himself entering their
conspiracy. Then he will learn the secrets. And he will come back
having achieved even more than they, for he is capable of working
harder, of being shrewder and of saving more quickly than any
of them.

MIGRANT TALKING TO VILLAGER, CALABRIA, ITALY

To be underdeveloped is not merely to be robbed or exploited: it is to be held in the grip of an artificial stasis. Underdevelopment not only kills: its essential stagnation denies life and resembles death. The migrant wants to live. It is not poverty alone that forces him to emigrate. Through his own individual effort he tries to achieve the dynamism that is lacking in the situation into which he was born.

One day he says he will leave. Until he said it, the decision was not really taken. When he has said it, it is known. The village knows. And the village then stands between him and his going back on his word. Some try to dissuade him. But they all recognize that he has decided. Until he said it, he had not decided.

He says good-bye to everyone. He leaves nobody out. He has known the village all his life. The intensity with which he feels this, at the moment of leaving, is almost as great as the force of his will. In leaving the village he chooses it as his own. The consequent confusion of feeling leads to questions. Will his uncle be alive when he returns? To say good-bye is to submit to the will of heaven. Who knows whether he will return triumphant or defeated? What the city offers is for those who succeed there, not for those who fail. He imagines the prizes of the city floating on

black water, in which those who lose will drown. The expressions on the village faces saying good-bye to him supply no answer.

He gives instructions about the land, the house, the well, the animals, as if in a few sentences he wished to re-perform the daily activity of years.

His mother has approved of his decision. It is a family matter and the family is going to benefit. But she hates the 'abroad' where he is going. And when it comes to his walking out of the house, she remembers how he was born. In the same room upstairs where she, her husband and her daughter still sleep. There were two women neighbours attending her, no doctor. The baby was a boy and his name had already been chosen. They gave him to her, and when she put him to her breast, he stopped crying. Now it is the moment of his departure. The two moments come together. She puts her two hands to either side of her head, rocking slightly on her feet – he is already shouting to the horse between the shafts of the cart – and it is as if, covering her head with her hands, she is holding in each ear the sounds of the twenty-five years which separate the two moments.

Without the example of a revolutionary party, the economic and social relations which create and maintain rural poverty, appear to be unchangeable. Therefore those with the most initiative do the one thing which seems to offer hope: they leave.

On the family cart to the nearest bus station there is not much left to say. They pass many people walking, riding, grazing cattle. The road itself is a passing of stories, with its listeners in the grass on either side.

It is the road along which as a boy with his brothers he tried to sell hazelnuts and wild strawberries to the occasional car that came from the market town.

Although monopoly capital succeeds in extracting super-profits, directly or indirectly, out of most of the people on earth, it does not transform most people in the world into industrial producers of surplus-value . . . Although it submits all classes and all nations (except those which have broken out of its realm) to various forms of common exploitation, it maintains and strengthens to the utmost the differences between these societies. Although the United States and India are more closely interwoven today than at any time in the past, the distance which separates their technology, their life-expectancy, their average culture, the way of living and of working of their inhabitants, is much wider today than it was a century ago, when there were hardly any relations at all between these two countries.

Only if we understand that imperialism brings to its widest possible application the universal law of uneven and combined development, can we understand world history in the twentieth century.

At the bus station he jumps down from the cart and says his last good-byes. The bus station – an assembly of wooden huts beside a large open parking space of mud and grass – is crowded. Those waiting sit or lie; others prepare to leave. The place is crowded too with the litter of the hours spent there. In the air a kind of residual cloud of sound, made up of words explaining and recounting journeys. There are families on the move from village to town or village to village. There are men coming home. There are other migrants. There are soldiers. He sits beside his suitcase and packages, which are tied tightly with string, knotted in many places. The packages contain what would not fit into the case, after-thoughts and last-minute presents. Inside them each solid object – cheese or razor – is carefully folded in cloth.

Modern industry has established the world market . . . This market has given an immense development to commerce, to navigation, to communication by land. This development has, in its turn, reacted on the extension of industry; and in proportion as industry, commerce, navigation, railways extended, in the same proportion the bourgeoisie developed, increased its capital, and pushed into the background every class handed down from the

Middle Ages. The bourgeoisie has subjected the country to the rule of the towns. It has created enormous cities, has greatly increased the urban population as compared with the rural, and has thus rescued a considerable part of the population from the idiocy of rural life. ('Communist Manifesto')

About the idiocy of rural life Marx exaggerated. Writing in 1848, he overestimated the capacity of urban rationality, and judged the village by the standards of the city.

The driver shouts something to the woman serving coffee in the buffet, sounds his klaxon, and the bus moves casually out on to the road, whose surface will slowly improve. At some moment on the way to the capital of his own country he will pass without realizing it the last of some species of animal or bird that he will not see for months: the last stork, the last mule, the last black pig. On his return journey he will recognize the first of this species as a kind of sentinel.

He is setting out single-handed to complete a historic transformation which has been stopped short.

In most underdeveloped countries capitalism has had a peculiarly twisted career. Having lived through all the pains and frustrations of childhood, it never experienced the vigour and exuberance of youth, and began displaying at an early age all the grievous features of senility and decadence. To the dead weight of stagnation characteristic of pre-industrial society was added the entire restrictive impact of monopoly capitalism. The economic surplus appropriated in lavish amounts by monopolistic concerns in backward countries is not employed for productive purposes. It is neither ploughed back into their own enterprises, nor does it serve to develop others. To the extent that it is not taken abroad by foreign stockholders, it is used in a manner very much resembling that of the landed aristocracy. It supports luxurious living by its recipients, is spent on construction of urban and rural residences, on servants, excess consumption and the like. The remainder is invested in the acquisition of rent-bearing land, in financing mercantile activities of all kinds, in usury and speculation. Last but not least, significant sums are removed abroad where they are held

GENTLEMEN'S CLUB, SEVILLE, SPAIN

as hedges against the depreciation of the domestic currency or as nest eggs assuring the owners suitable retreats in the case of social and political upheavals at home.

A Portuguese migrant: 'You know what it's like in our country? There are many capitalists and they keep their money and do nothing with it, they keep it. It's like digging a hole, putting the money in it, filling up the hole and never uncovering it.'

The migrant inherits poverty. But that is too generally expressed to reveal the drama of his situation. The items of his inheritance need to be listed.

Penetration of Western capital into his country
(within the memory of his grandfather)
Destruction of pre-capitalist rural self-sufficiency
Reinforcement of semi-feudal landowning class
Production of raw materials, cash crops, etc., for foreign interest
Rise of local merchant capital
Rapid growth of a few industries under monopoly conditions

Result:

Local industrial development ⎫
General technological development ⎪
Land reform ⎬ **Blocked**
Modern agriculture ⎭

Commodity circulation
Diffusion of metropolitan culture
Population increase (due to improved medicine)
Absolute polarization between rich and poor
Alliance between merchant capital, landowners and foreign
interests against any threat of social change

Result:

Modern education ⎫
Securalization of life ⎬ **Blocked**
Political democracy ⎭

Turkey in 1967 had a population of thirty-four million growing at the rate of 3 per cent each year. 80 per cent of the population were peasants. 90 per cent of the agriculture was entirely unmechanized. Of the industry which existed 60 per cent produced only food, wine and tobacco. The entire industrial sector contributed only 15 per cent of the GNP (Gross National Product). There were one million unemployed. And about four million in the countryside who could only find work at harvest time. Each year three hundred thousand more workers came on to the labour market. Nearly 70 per cent of the population could neither read nor write. By 1967 there were about a quarter of a million Turkish migrants working abroad. Today (1974) there are more than three times that number.

The bus is in the suburbs of the capital of his country. He sees an agglomeration of small improvised lean-to dwellings constructed from spare bricks, scrapwood and discarded corrugated iron. In these live the villagers who have reached the capital and have gone no further.

The city is larger than he imagined, with more people. He is conscious of the will which is required to pass through it. Nearly everyone speaks the same language as he does, uses the same words; yet there are already unfamiliar things: kinds of fish such as he has never before seen on sale in the market: extravagant tableware in a shop window: cakes and sweetmeats in strange forms. Increasingly what he encounters will be unfamiliar. He sees many others like himself, who have come this far and then stopped.

Like all the swollen capitals of underdeveloped countries, Athens is not an industrial town despite its size and growth. Less than a third of its registered 'active' population is employed in industry. Of these, almost a half are employed in units of less than ten persons, usually family enterprises of a primitive character.

The crowd in the large piazza by the station is like a map of the whole country's villages dramatically shifted so that the distances between them have been reduced to a few yards. What holds them together are rumours and propositions. A kind of trade is going on. Not with commodities but with opportunities, real or fictitious: the chance of a part-time job: the promise of a word dropped in such-and-such an office: a contact for a cheap ticket: the loan of the capital necessary to buy a weighing machine.

The capital necessary to buy a weighing machine. The kind made for bathrooms, with a rubber platform for bare wet feet. With luck a second-hand one. But it must register accurately. To wrap it up in paper and go to a street near the station and to sit there on the pavement with the weighing machine now unwrapped and on display. And there to cry out all day long: Your weight! Your true weight! A few will stop to have themselves weighed for fear that they are putting on too much fat. A few more out of idle curiosity. Throughout the whole day of crying: Your weight! Your true weight! to collect – if there are not too many others working the same street – enough money to buy food for one person in the evening.

A man's resolution to emigrate needs to be seen within the context of a world economic system. Not in order to reinforce a political theory but so that what actually happens to him can be given its proper value. That economic system is neo-colonialism. Economic theory can show how this system, creating under-development, produces the conditions which lead to emigration: it can also show why the system needs the special labour power which the migrant workers have to sell. Yet necessarily the language of economic theory is abstract. And so, if the forces which determine the migrant's life are to be grasped and realized as part of his personal destiny, a less abstract formulation is needed. Metaphor is needed. Metaphor is temporary. It does not replace theory.

The migrant takes with him his own resolution, the food prepared in his home, which he will eat during the next two or three days, his own pride, the photographs in his pocket, his packages, his suitcase.

Yet his migration is like an event in a dream dreamt by another. As a figure in a dream dreamt by an unknown sleeper, he appears to act autonomously, at times unexpectedly; but everything he does – unless he revolts – is determined by the needs of the dreamer's mind. Abandon the metaphor. The migrant's intentionality is permeated by historical necessities of which neither he nor anybody he meets is aware. That is why it is as if his life were being dreamt by another.

A Turk: 'For six months a year in the countryside you sleep because there is no work and you are poor.'

At some point he crossed the frontier. This may or may not have coincided with the geographical frontier of his country. It isn't the geographical frontier that counts: the frontier is simply where he is liable to be stopped and his intention to leave thwarted. On the far side of the frontier, when he has crossed it, he becomes a migrant worker. He might have crossed it in a dozen ways. Here are three ways of describing a crossing:

A Turkish peasant, who failed to pass the official medical examination, decided to enter Germany as a tourist. But a Turk in a crowded train, who says he is a tourist, may have to prove himself to the frontier police by showing what currency or cheques he has on him. And so the peasant bought a first-class ticket to Cologne, confident that in a first-class compartment he would have the air of being wealthy enough not to be questioned. He crossed the frontier.

SPANISH MOUNTAINSIDE

Until recently most emigration from Portugal was illegal. Both the Spanish and French frontiers had to be crossed clandestinely. Smugglers in Lisbon arranged such crossings. Their fee was $350 per person. Having paid this sum, many would-be migrants were cheated. They were led into the mountains just across the Spanish frontier and left there. Totally disorientated, some died of starvation and exposure: some found their way back, $350 the poorer. ($350 at this time represented as much as a year's earnings for the average Portuguese peasant. In 1964 the average per capita income in Portugal – an average which included the incomes of the upper class – was \$370.) So the migrants devised a system to protect themselves. Before leaving they had their photographs taken. They tore the photograph in half, giving one

half to their 'guide' and keeping the other themselves. When they reached France they sent their half of the photograph back to their family in Portugal to show that they had been safely escorted across the frontiers; the 'guide' came to the family with his half of the photograph to prove that it was he who had escorted them, and it was only then that the family paid the \$350. The migrants crossed in groups of a hundred or so. Mostly they travelled by night. Hidden in lorries. And on foot.

After nine days he reached Paris. He had the address of a Portuguese friend, but he knew no directions. To find the address he must take a taxi. Before letting him open the door, the taxi driver asked to see his money. A policeman was standing near by. Both policeman and taxi driver agreed that to go to the shanty town of Saint-Denis the passenger must pay double. He did not ask why. He was a newly arrived migrant who could not afford not to take a taxi and could not afford to argue. He too had crossed the frontier.

From Istanbul the majority of migrants go to Germany. Their crossing of the frontier is officially organized. They go to the Recruitment Centre. There they are medically examined and undergo tests to prove that they possess the skills which they claim to have. Those who pass, sign a contract immediately with the German firm which is going to employ them. Then they get into a labour train and travel for three days. When they arrive they are met by representatives of the German firm and taken to their lodgings and the factory.

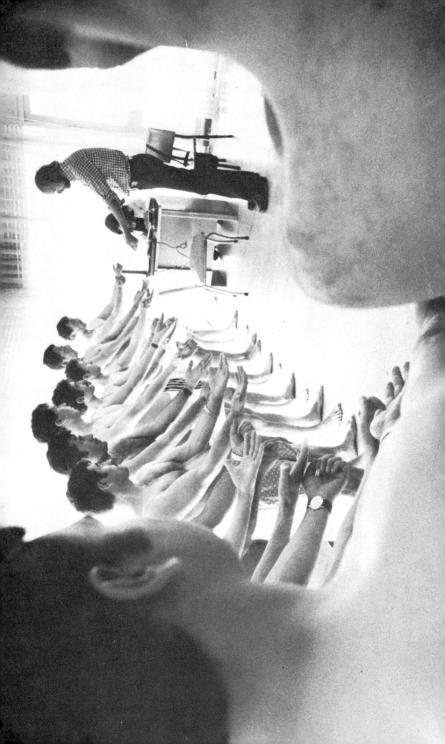

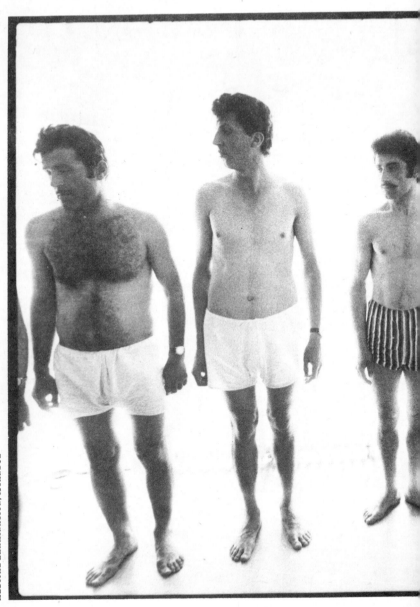

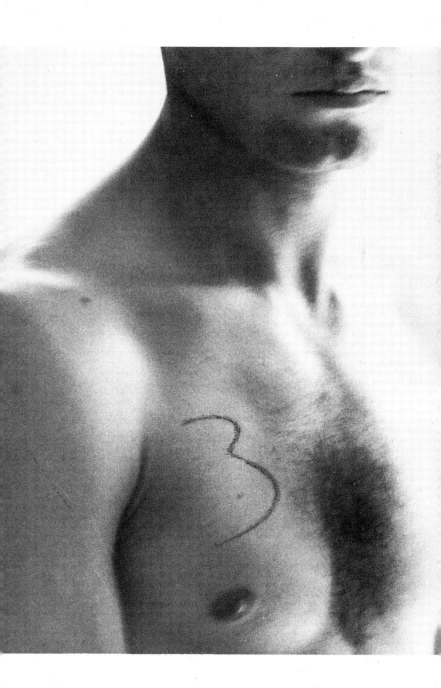

He strips and lines up with many hundreds of other
novice migrants. They glance hastily (to stare would be to show
their astonishment) at the implements and machines being used to
examine them. Also hastily at one another, each trying to compare
his chances with those around him. Nothing has prepared him for
this situation. It is unprecedented. And yet it is already normal.
The humiliating demand to be naked before strangers. The
incomprehensible language spoken by the officials in command.
The meaning of the tests. The numerals written on their bodies with
felt pens. The rigid geometry of the room. The women in overalls
like men. The smell of an unknown liquid medicine. The silence of
so many like himself. The in-turned look of the majority which yet
is not a look of calm or prayer. If it has become normal, it is
because the momentous is happening without exception to them all.

MEDICAL TEST, ISTANBUL

TAP FACTORY, SWITZERLAND

53

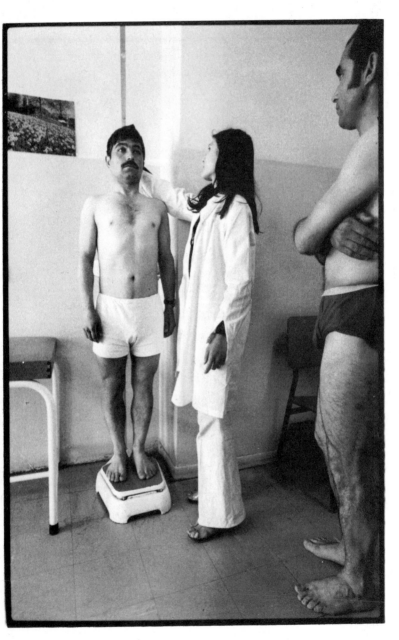

TURKISH WORKER BEING MEASURED, ISTANBUL. HE FAILED EXAMINATION BECAUSE HE WAS NOT TALL ENOUGH

The fit are being sorted from the unfit. One in five will fail. Those who pass will enter a new life. The machines are examining what is invisible inside their bodies. Some have waited eight years for this chance of crossing.

A man asks him if there is a machine which can reveal what he fears is a kind of disease in his head: the disease of not being able to read.

GERMAN DOCTOR AT RECRUITMENT CENTRE, ISTANBUL, SHOWING HIS 'MUSEUM'. THE COLLECTION CONSISTS OF VESSELS, BOTTLES, WATER PISTOLS, CONFISCATED FROM THOSE APPLYING FOR WORK IN GERMANY. OUTSIDE THE RECRUITMENT CENTRE WOULD-BE MIGRANTS CAN BUY 'GOOD' URINE ON THE BLACK MARKET; THEY DO SO BECAUSE THEY FEAR THEIR OWN MAY BE UNHEALTHY. THEY PUT THE BOUGHT URINE INTO VESSELS LIKE THE ONES CONFISCATED, AND TRY TO SUBSTITUTE IT FOR THEIR OWN WHEN ASKED FOR A SPECIMEN

A VILLAGE MASON TAKING A TRADE TEST IN BRICK-LAYING AT RECRUITMENT CENTRE, ISTANBUL. HE FAILED

When the medical tests are finished, there are tests of skill to qualify for the job. Show how strong you are, a friend had advised, answer slowly, and show how strong you are. Some sit to wait for the results. Others pace. The expression on many faces is reminiscent of another situation: the expression of a father waiting outside whilst his child is being born. Here he awaits his own new life.

TURKISH WORKERS ABOUT TO BE TOLD WHETHER THEY HAVE PASSED THEIR MEDICAL AND TRADE TESTS

He passed and was born.

What distinguishes this migration from others in the past is that it is temporary. Only a minority of workers are permitted to settle permanently in the country to which they have come. Their work contracts are usually for one year, or, at the most, two. The migrant worker comes to sell his labour power where there is a labour shortage. He is admitted to do a certain kind of job. He has no rights, claims, or reality outside his filling of that job. While he fills it, he is paid and accommodated. If he no longer does so, he is sent back to where he came from. It is not men who immigrate but machine-minders, sweepers, diggers, cement mixers, cleaners, drillers, etc. This is the significance of temporary migration. To re-become a man (husband, father, citizen, patriot) a migrant has to return home. The home he left because it held no future for him.

In one of the packages and stuffed down in the corner of his suitcase, is the food he has brought. He thinks of it – the

hard sausage to be sliced with the knife, the crumbling cheese – while the countryside and towns pass by the train window. The need to eat is not an expression of hunger. Food is also a kind of message. To eat it, is to receive a message. Sent by whom from where? At this moment the answer is simple. He begins to eat before he is hungry. Some eat as much as they can: others try to space out the messages from the past throughout the long journey.

After twenty-four hours, the bouts of sleep get more spasmodic and the hours of being awake slightly less clear. The train becomes like a field of runners a long way after the start, when they are spaced out and separated and no two of them are in the same place running at the same speed. A man, middle-aged, with a large moustache, who sits in the middle of the carriage, his hands firmly placed on his knees, sings a few bars of a song at the same moment as the thin man beside him is falling asleep, and the one opposite is absent-mindedly cleaning his teeth with the point of his knife. Even in the card games there is a spacing out of the players. His attention is wandering. With all his energy he concentrates on the new deal, as if it too were a refrain from a song. Then he actually breaks into song, throws in the cards as soon as the hand is finished, and falls asleep until his head topples and rests on the shoulder of his neighbour. And all the time, sideways, countryside and towns are passing the window.

The future of the next few days contains so many unknowns that any sense of continuous time stops short before it, or makes a detour around it. Envisaged, the future about to begin is a wall, not a space: a wall not unlike the wall of an ancient city, except that its surface is not time-honoured and hand-cut but time-defying and like the surface of a television screen behind which random images appear, yet which, when empty, is an opaque cloud that nothing can penetrate. In his half sleep he approaches the wall and searches for an entrance. Later, he turns his back on it and remembers the last few days.

DEPARTURE, ISTANBUL

61

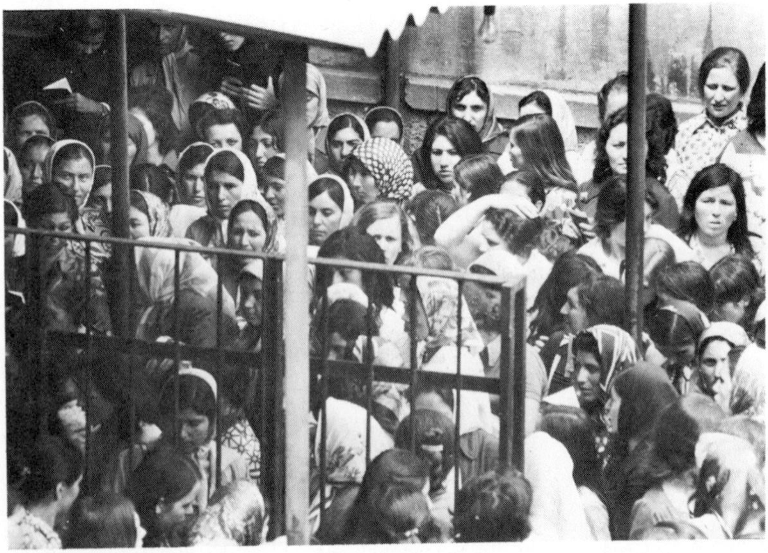

DEPARTURE, RAILWAY STATION, ISTANBUL

DEPARTURE, RAILWAY STATION, ISTANBUL

They are coming to offer their labour. Their labour power is ready-made. The industrialized country, whose production is going to benefit from it, has not borne any of the cost of creating it; any more than it will bear the cost of supporting a seriously sick migrant worker, or one who has grown too old to work. So far as the economy of the metropolitan country is concerned, migrant workers are immortal: immortal because continually interchangeable. They are not born: they are not brought up: they do not age: they do not get tired: they do not die. They have a single function – to work. All other functions of their lives are the responsibility of the country they come from.

Migrant workers, already living in the metropolis, have the habit of visiting the main railway station. To talk in groups there, to watch the trains come in, to receive first-hand news from their country, to anticipate the day when they will begin the return journey.

In his imagination every migrant worker is in transit. He remembers the past: he anticipates the future: his aims and his recollections make his thoughts a train between the two.

In the winter the main railway station is warm. And it is one of the few places where events occur and they can remain spectators, and at the same time outnumber the citizens. The constituents of leisure: the right to watch, and the capacity to be at ease with those of your own choosing.

He is listening to the noise of the train in the throat of the journey. The noise is as regular as the lines. Over this, irregularly, rising to crescendos and falling away, are the noises of what the train is passing: the fields murmur, brick walls pound fists on metal, a station throws gravel against the windows. When the terminus first arrives, it does so in silence.

The packages and suitcases are handed out through the windows to those who have already got down on to the platform. The train empties. The station extends over and around them. Everything, except for themselves getting their baggage out of the train, appears to be ordered and in its place. Except for them. The uniforms of the officials with their gold braid and eagles and burning torches are similar to ones they have seen before. It is the clothes of the few civilians which are startling. And more than their clothes, their expressions. They look as though they are not using their eyes, and yet they walk quickly.

Once more he is under the grey cloud-coloured wall like a television screen on which bright images flicker, and from which new unfamiliar sounds are emitted. The wall will divide and they will enter this time. They are led off the platform to a Reception Centre. Behind the sound of their own excited speech comes the clipped noise of an incomprehensible language. The loudspeakers speak their own language but as if linen was tied tight across the mouth of the woman speaking. They would prefer it not to be a woman. Who is she? Who is telling her what to say? The written letters of the other language are jumbled together to make silent sounds.

SCHOKOLADE IST GUT!

The silence is his. Whatever they are saying, he, with the silent sounds in his head, is going to nod.

They trail through halls higher than many trees. They form a single file to go up an escalator. It is impossible to tell which is ground level. An official shouts and points when a suitcase scrapes against the side. They file down corridors, through glass doors, before grilles. By looking at each other, they realize how dishevelled and rough they have become in comparison with the strangers who are dealing with them. But equally this is a reminder of their achievement. They have crossed the frontier.

Arriving alone, the shock of the birth of his new life is immediate. He calls upon each year of his manhood in order not to panic. In a group it is easier.

In a group they arrive like a band. They tell each other by word and gesture that they are stronger and have more stamina and more cunning than the inhabitants of the foreign city.

A French peasant: Nobody wants to live in the country any more. In the city they dress like princes; they drive their cars; and they see nothing and they understand nothing. My system is to study everything: nature, plants, animals (including us) and the climate.

Everything looks new. The way people walk and move about at different levels, as though each level was unmistakably the ground. The surfaces walked on, or touched. The unusual sound which a usual movement makes. The seamless joints between things. Even glass looks different here, thicker and less brittle. The newness of the substance of things combines with the incomprehensibility of the language.

polystyrene	lön
övertid	cellulose acetate
epok	arbetstillstand
dödsfall	glass fibre

Trams passed one another, ingoing, outgoing, clanging. Useless words. Things go on the same; day after day: squads of police marching out, back; trams in, out . . . Cityful passing away, other cityful coming, passing away too: other coming on, passing on. Houses, lines of houses, streets, miles of pavements, piled-up bricks, stones.

Around the exit men were talking in his own language. The words of it are like foliage re-appearing on a tree after winter. He recognized a man he already knew at home. The second man had been working in the metropolis for two years. They embraced everything which was familiar in the other. They repeated each other's names and the names of their villages. Then, full of the excitement of arrival, he said: 'Here you can find gold on the ground. I am going to start looking for it.' The friend who had been in the city for two years answered him: 'That is true. But the gold fell from very high in the sky, and so when it hit the earth, it went down very very deep'.

Migration involves the transfer of a valuable economic resource – human labour – from the poor to the rich countries. The workers who migrate may have been unemployed in the country of origin, but this does not alter the fact that the community has

MIGRANT WORKERS ARRIVING AT GENEVA STATION

invested considerable sums in their upbringing. Economists sometimes speak of 'emigration as capital export' similar to the export of other factors of production. It has been estimated that the upbringing, the price of survival till the age of twenty of a migrant, has cost the national economy of his own country about £2,000. With each migrant who arrives, an underdeveloped economy is subsidizing a developed one to that amount. Yet the saving for the industrialized country is even greater. Given its higher standard of living, the cost of 'producing' an eighteen-year-old worker at home is between £8,000 and £16,000.

The use of labour, already produced elsewhere, means an annual saving for the metropolitan countries of £8,000 million.

To those who have machines, men are given.

PASSPORT CONTROL, GENEVA

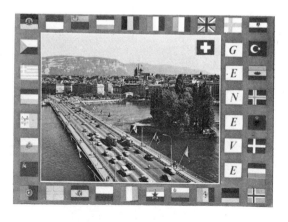

Apologists for the system argue that the advantages are mutual. According to them, emigration benefits the under-developed country in the following ways:

1. Emigration reduces population pressure. Young migrants marry later. Married migrants – absent from their wives – procreate less.

2. Emigration reduces unemployment and raises wages. Further, a shortage of labour in the migrant's country of origin will encourage mechanization.

MIGRANT WORKERS LEAVING RECEPTION CENTRE FOR CITY, GENEVA

3. The migrants acquire industrial skills to take home with them.
Their experience in industry is educative.

4. The remittances the migrants send home improve their country's

balance of payments. (In 1972 the remittances sent home by migrant workers in Germany totalled at least $3 billion.) These remittances help to supply capital for local industrial investment.

Behind this curtain of argument, the distant reality remains unchanged:

1. Migrants are the most enterprising of their generation.

2. Their labour is lost to their own country.

3. If local unemployment is reduced, it usually means whole areas losing nearly all their able-bodied men. Around the 'ghost villages' cultivation deteriorates further.

4. The moneyed classes in an underdeveloped economy have little interest in industrial or agricultural mechanization.

5. Migrants remain unskilled workers. They learn their new job in a few days.

6. When they return home, the factories have not been built.

7. The underdeveloped countries are in debt to the developed countries – hence their balance-of-payments problem. Migrants' remittances are deposited in banks who lend this money back to the developed countries. When the remittances are withdrawn from the banks, a large part of them is spent on the purchase of further commodities from the developed countries.

The gold fell from very high in the sky, and so when it hit the earth, it went down very very deep.

2.WORK

This city is exceptional.
It was built vertically
and does not stand on the earth.
It grew like ivy on a wall.
We who live in it walk
up and down
with the ease of centipedes.
At right angles
to the plain and sea
we live on the walls of a shaft.
A river runs between our streets
like rain down bark.

The last day of the year
all cities have the right
to wear disguise.
With immunity Marrakech
can put on the clothes of Paris
Madrid can imagine itself free
Trinidad blow up the Bank of England.

This city invents for itself
a sky
unwinds it like a bale of cloth

In a dream I found

Wo
Bro

and the
a measu
of a futu

Ye
reconstr
resourc
face har

To
estant, t
cism. Th
erarchy
and the
were reg
immigra

a bird's egg the blue of the sky.
Where the blue joins the roofs of the street
it rattles inaudibly.
my eyes see the sound.

At the core of the sun
in the sky
the glacier of justice may attain
the speed of light
taking a month
to cross the solar system
or a hundred thousand years
to reach the farthest star
within our galaxy.

At the end of the street
a sparrow
perches high up against the sky
in a tree of veins
near the cortex.

When a prisoner is shot
the sparrow flies
out of his eyes.

The sky today
is milling with invisible survivors.
From the shaft we wave.

He has come to the metropolis to sell his labour power.

All the industrial countries of Europe employ and
depend upon migrant labour. Three quarters of those who arrive go
to the two largest: France and Germany. At first the migrant
worker chooses according to his local tradition. If he is Turkish he
is likely to go to Germany; if he is Portuguese, to France; if he is
Greek he may go to Sweden.

He is free to sell his labour power like a commodity.

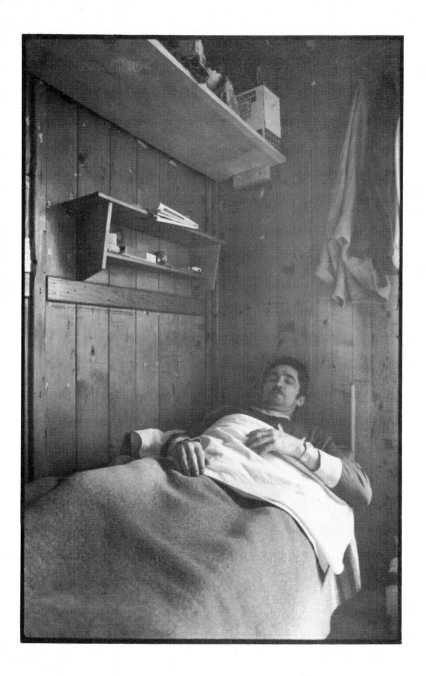

Two thirds work in industry, building or construction. (It is he who has built the roads which will lead him to a new life. Roads, autoroutes, tunnels, airstrips, fly-overs.) A few work in agriculture. The rest in the service sector. In France 20 per cent of all industrial workers are migrants: in Germany 12 per cent: in Switzerland 40 per cent. They are concentrated in the hardest, most disagreeable and less well-paid jobs, for example in the plastics, rubber and asbestos processing industries in Germany. On the assembly line of the Ford factory in Cologne 40 per cent of the labour force are migrants: in the Renault workshops in France 40 per cent; in the Volvo factory in Gothenburg 45 per cent.

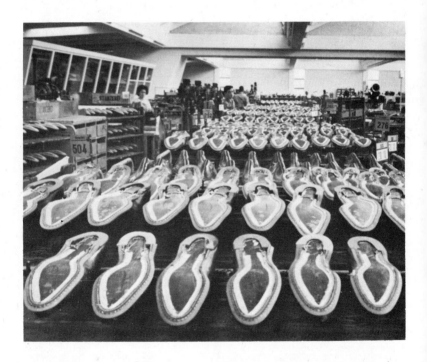

To live he can sell his life.

The firm he has already contracted to work for is supplying him with a bed in a room. Over half of all migrant workers live in company lodgings or barracks.

One of the walls of the corner where his bed is, leads
to a door, the door opens on to a passage, at the end of the passage
are the taps to wash under and the place he can shit in, the wet
floor of this place leads to the way out, down the stairs into the
street, along the walls of the buildings on one side and the wall
of the traffic on the other, past the railings, under the glass and
artificial light to the work he does: that floor to clean: that hole to
punch: that ingot to lift: that casing to beat: that gearbox to fit in;
the job done, an identical or almost identical job takes its place,
the same job, but a different floor, a different hole, a different ingot,
a different casing, a different gearbox; they must be different
because he has just done the job, and now he has to do it again,
and after that again and again. They must be different and they

look the same: they are joined one to another across the city in
which everything is joined, in which everything is continuous,
beginning from the wall in the corner of the room where his bed is.
Everything is part of the same thing: at one bit he works, along
another bit he walks, in another bit he sleeps, at another bit which
is shaped like a table he eats, and what he eats are edible bits. All
the bits are parts of the same thing which he is now in, and in

which, if he makes a wrong movement or a false step, he will be crushed; there is just enough place in it for him to do what he is told how to do, but there is no room for anything else, except in his bed to sleep.

In France, until recently 80 per cent of migrant workers lived illegally without papers. This constituted an 'official' unofficial system. Migrants could sometimes legalize their position if they found a job and accommodation and their employer supported them. By initially making migrants law-breakers the system had the advantage of emphasizing from the start that they had no inalienable rights – only rights that might later be earned. Today the government claims that the situation is being regularized. But without doubt many migrants – perhaps as many as half if one includes those who come from former French colonies in Africa – still arrive without papers.

In Germany where all legal immigration is organized by a state agency (firms who want migrants pay a fee of $392 per head to the agency for bringing him in), there are between a quarter and a half million migrant workers who have been smuggled in or, more rarely, have smuggled themselves in.

ILLEGAL MIGRANT

He arrived without papers. When the greetings were over, he looked at his cousin inquiringly, without saying a word. Outside in the unheard of streets there were shouts he did not understand. His cousin bared his teeth in a grimace which was only half joke. Now you are here, you can see what it is like. The cup is chipped. They are always on our backs. But you will go home successful. It was said encouragingly and conspiratorially.

After a few days in the room with his cousin and seven others, he has to find work and lodging. They will help him when they hear of a job. But it may take time and he is already short of money. He has paid his fare and the bribes with money he borrowed before he left. Outside a factory where he has been told there are no jobs, a man appears in the street, walks by his side and speaks his language like a compatriot. The man says he can find him a job.

An illegal migrant worker cannot go to the labour office. He cannot read the foreign papers. And so there is a trafficking by middle-men who read the announcements in the papers and sell the information to the newly arrived migrant. When he gets the job, he pays the middle-man two weeks' wages.

He is not lacking in cunning. When he bargained in a cattle market, he tried to get the best of the deal and the deal was a highly complicated battle of wits: a contest about the direction from which he could persuade the other to approach the truth (and therefore see only part of it), and about the safeguarding of an 'honourable' way back for himself if the other happened to unmask his cunning.

The city confidence-trick is different. It works on the assumption that strangers never meet twice and that anything may be called true because the city, like the sea, covers everything and everybody. The confidence-trick runs endlessly parallel to life; its terms are similar to those experienced in a state of hypnosis: the trickster is always between his victim and reality.

The man gives him, in a confidential whisper, the address of a tile factory. He is taken on at a wage of £17 a week. A legal migrant may earn £40 to £50 a week. He still considers himself lucky. He can work every day. If he works overtime or at nights, he will be able to save. Later he will look for another job. His being in the metropolis is still a prize: a prize he is frightened of losing. One false move with his employer or with somebody quite unknown in the street and he risks being discovered and sent home. He must continually safeguard the prize.

Look for lodgings. His cousin and the seven others have told him where to try. The first door opens and immediately frames an unknown person. He asks in five words learnt by heart. He imagined the reply to his question would be an action, an opening of a room door, the handing over of some money. Instead the unknown person stares at him with an unknowable expression, the expression of something that continually jerks up and down behind the skin of the face like an evil jack-in-the-box, and which he on the doorstep can only glimpse through the eyes of the face when it reaches the top of its jump, before it goes down to come up again a few words later. Behind the person, beyond the corridor and the mystery of its arrangements, are the unknown person's unknown reasons for shutting the door while still speaking.

Peasants are hard, cunning and often two-faced. In the dark, lest he be seen, a man plots – slowly, obstinately – his own revenge. The dark he does this in, is like a kind of sleep: there is room for only one person in it. The village is vindictive. The feeble are mocked. The powerful are flattered. There is no need to idealize the village. But sometimes something happens on an ordinary day in a village which never happens in a city. (Revolution or siege may confer this possibility upon the city.) A man or a woman acts altruistically. A spontaneous action, quite uncalculated. A protest against an injustice suffered by somebody else. An offer which is really a sacrifice. And this action provokes an echo, becomes resonant. An echo from where? The sky? The fields? Ancestors? The village tower? The echo is inaudible but it completes the act. The one who acts feels it, and some who witness the action feel it too. In the metropolis no action can be completed in this way.

Those who let out the most miserable rooms to migrant workers are called sleep-dealers (marchands de sommeil). In a small room for one person (a maid's room a century ago) three beds have been arranged. Nine men sleep in these three beds by the arrangement of working different shifts: three per twenty-four hours. He pays £8 a month – or one tenth of his salary.

lpes l'étoile

,00 *
2,55
2,20
2,35
1,40
1,42
9,92 *

He shops in a supermarket for the first time.

The extent of what is there, mysteriously there – for most of it is packaged and since he cannot read the labels he is by no means certain of the contents – is far greater than the goods in all the houses of the village if they were assembled together in a single place and put on shelves. People walk slowly past these shelves and occasionally take a package. It looks as though they are stealing. Their total lack of expression suggests a kind of cunning. Yet they are not furtive. He hesitates to do the same: he may be accused of being a thief. There are things to eat and things to use. He sees some tomatoes, ordinary tomatoes, in a pannier. He resolves to take them, also some bread. He follows the others pushing silver carts. He hands over a note: coins fall out of the mouth of a machine into a metal dewlap. The woman behind pushes and points that he should pick up the change. Back in his bed he calculates slowly and methodically how much the purchases have cost. He judges their price in relation to his first pay packet. He concludes that it will take him twice as long as he thought to achieve his savings. Unless he finds another job.

Figures converge from several directions on the factory gate. There are thousands, men and women, on foot, on bicycles, in cars. Their common destination forces them closer together until they are standing shoulder to shoulder. Yet, apart from a few brief greetings, they seem scarcely to notice one another; each is lost in his own thoughts, as if everyone had received that morning a separate message which had compelled him to come.

Before they clock in, whilst they are still outside, capable of simply turning round and walking away; their air of estrangement from one another is so strong that it makes him wonder whether they are not all new migrant workers like himself from different countries.

To try to understand the experience of another it is

necessary to dismantle the world as seen from one's own place within it, and to reassemble it as seen from his. For example, to understand a given choice another makes, one must face in imagination the lack of choices which may confront and deny him. The well-fed are incapable of understanding the choices of the under-fed. The world has to be dismantled and re-assembled in order to be able to grasp, however clumsily, the experience of another. To talk of entering the other's subjectivity is misleading. The subjectivity of another does not simply constitute a different interior attitude to the same exterior facts. The constellation of facts, of which he is the centre, is different.

He is taught his work. When he can do it, he will earn £40 a week if he works overtime. He watches the gestures made and he learns to imitate them. Words would involve somebody speaking his language.

Modern mass production presupposes that most of the labour involved in it is unskilled. In the mid-twenties Henry Ford declared that 79 per cent of his workers could learn their job in eight days, and that 43 per cent of them could do so in one day. It is the same today.

ROAD TO VILLAGE IN SPAIN

The history of the last two centuries, if the apologetics are put aside, is nothing less than infernal. It is hard to credit that it was exactly during this period that the notion of Evil as a force was abandoned. Every child in developed Europe who goes to school learns something, however mystified and prejudiced the school books may be, of the previous history of capitalism: the slave trade, the Poor Laws, child labour, factory conditions, the Armageddon of 1914–18. Faced with this record, the capitalist system claims that it has evolved and that the inhumanities of the past can never be repeated. This claim is implicit in all public communications: we live – so we are taught – in a democratic system which respects human rights. The excesses of the past were incidental to the true nature of the system.

They watch the gestures made and they learn to imitate them. The single gesture may not in itself demand great effort, but the repetition by which gesture is laid upon gesture, precisely but inexorably, the pile of gestures being stacked minute by minute, hour by hour, is exhausting. The rate of work allows no time to prepare for the gesture, to demand an effort from the body. The body loses its mind in the gesture.

WOMAN MIGRANT WORKER IN FACTORY, LYON

1. Pick up bottles (2 rows of 3).

   Grasp 6 bottles (2 in left hand, 4 in right hand). Hold thumbs toward you and fingers away from you.

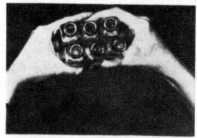

2. Inspect necks.

   Tilt necks slightly so that the light will show defects.

3. Separate bottles.

   Separate bottles so that the left hand holds 2 and the right hand 4.

4. Turn left wrist to left with palm of hand up. At the same time move the left thumb toward the left so that the top bottle falls into place to the left of the bottom bottle. This places 2 bottles in the palm ready for inspection. Use the left thumb as a stop.

Fig. 327. Pictorial instruction sheet for inspection of bottles

Improved working and living conditions, social welfare, parliamentary democracy, the benefits of modern technology are cited to substantiate the claim that the inhumanities of the past were incidental. In the metropolitan centres the claim is generally believed. The most naked forms of exploitation are invisible there because they occur in the antipodes of the Third World. The antipodes are cultural as well as geographical. A 'bidonville' outside Páris belongs to them. The migrants who sleep buried in cellars belong to them. They are there, but they are not seen.

Meanwhile, the indigenous worker has been made a consumer in the hope that the latter will console the former for the unfreedom of his work. A British worker at Fords: 'You don't achieve anything here. A robot could do it. The line here is made for morons. It doesn't need any thought. They tell you that. "We don't pay you for thinking" they say. Everyone comes to realize that they're not doing a worthwhile job. They're just on the line. For the money. Nobody likes to think that they're a failure. It's bad when you know that you're just a little cog. You just look at your pay packet – you look at what it does for your wife and kids. That's the only answer.'

He begins to watch his arm, as if it were being moved by what it is holding instead of by his shoulder. He thinks of water pumping his arm. The moving pieces shift his eyes, the air breathes his lungs. In places liquids ooze out of the machine like the liquid that gathers round a fish's mouth when it has been taken out of the water and has stopped thrashing. He knows that what he is doing is separate from any skill he has. He can stuff a saddle with straw. He has been told that the factory makes washing machines.

It is difficult to grasp a 'normal', familiar situation
as a whole: rather, one reacts with a series of habitual responses,
which, although they are reactions, really belong to that situation.
History, political theory, sociology can help one to understand
that 'the normal' is only normative. Unfortunately these
disciplines are usually used to do the opposite: to serve tradition by
asking questions in such a way that the answers sanctify the norms
as absolutes. Every tradition forbids the asking of certain questions
about what has really happened to you.

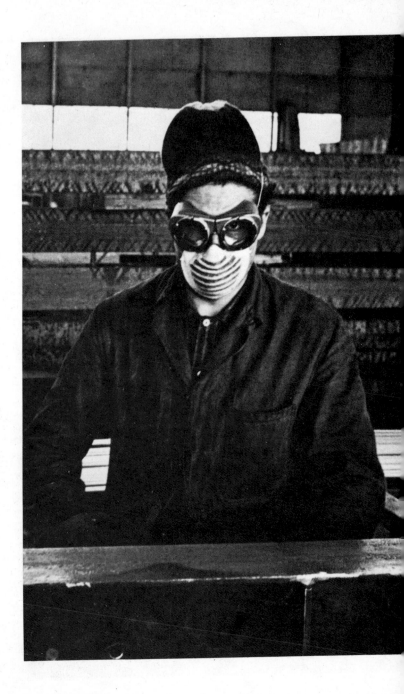

The 'normal' is only fully exposed for what it is through action which opposes it, ie, 'abnormal', 'extremist', or revolutionary action. When the normal is thus stripped of its normalcy, one's proper sense of being exceptional extends beyond oneself to the entire historical moment in which one is living.

I then recognize what is being done to me, as well as what I do; and I discover how much of myself the 'normal' denies or suppresses.

To see the experience of another, one must do more than dismantle and reassemble the world with him at its centre. One must interrogate his situation to learn about that part of his experience which derives from the historical moment. What is being done to him, even with his own complicity, under the cover of normalcy? Is what is being done to him new?

Marx (1867): In the factory we have a lifeless mechanism independent of the workman, who becomes its mere living appendage . . . at the same time that factory works exhausts the nervous system to the uttermost, it does away with the many-sided play of muscles, and confiscates every atom of freedom, both in bodily and in intellectual activity.

Stamping, boring, pressing, beating, the scream of hydraulic tools, the shock of substance hitting substance, and one substance grating against another. It takes him a long time to get accustomed to the noise. The noise itself hits and grates against further substances. Within the reverberations there are insistent rhythms so that every echo is interrupted before it is finished; nothing dies away and nothing begins. If the noise slackens or if he leaves the workshop, its cessation does not bring a stillness because the same insistent, amputated rhythms are still present in his head and, since he feels these and can hear nothing, it is like going deaf.

Silence here is deafness.

Marx (1867): Every organ of sense is injured in an equal degree by artificial elevation of the temperature, by the dust-laden atmosphere, by the deafening noise, not to mention

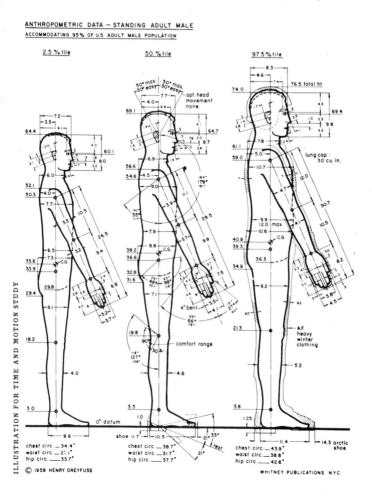

ANTHROPOMETRIC DATA — STANDING ADULT MALE
ACCOMMODATING 95% OF U.S. ADULT MALE POPULATION

ILLUSTRATION FOR TIME AND MOTION STUDY

© 1959 HENRY DREYFUSS

WHITNEY PUBLICATIONS N.Y.C.

danger to life and limb among the thickly crowded machinery, which, with the regularity of the seasons, issues its list of the killed and wounded in the industrial battle.

Henry Ford (1922): I have not been able to discover that repetitive labour injures a man in any way. I have been told by parlour experts that repetitive labour is soul- as well as body-destroying, but that has not been the result of our investigations. There was one case of a man who all day long did little but step on

a treadle release. He thought that the motion was making him one-sided; the medical examination did not show that he had been affected but, of course, he was changed to another job that used a different set of muscles. In a few weeks he asked for his old job again. It would seem reasonable to imagine that going through the same set of motions daily for eight hours would produce an abnormal body, but we have never had a case of it.

His senses are assailed by the irregularity of what they experience, but if he looks around he can see nothing that is irregular – as the leaves of a tree are irregular, as the way any animal walks is irregular – except in what is disused or strained: the liquids on the floor, the scraps of discarded material, the backs of his own hands, the face of the man beside him. The strangeness of it all makes him think at first that the job involves more skill than it does. He projects the difficulty of his own adaptation on to the movements he has to make. Later when his surprise has run out, and two or three paths through the factory have become familiar to him, he becomes confident.

Whenever industrial cities have needed to enlarge or re-create a section of their proletariat (that section which is sometimes called a sub-proletariat because its wages are the lowest, its employment the least secure, and its labour the least skilled), peasants from the countryside have been drawn into the cities and transformed there into urban workers.

Just as agencies now in Istanbul or Athens or Zagreb arrange contracts whereby workers go to Cologne or Brussels, so in early nineteenth-century Britain, agents were set up by the Poor Law Commissions to recruit the unemployed in the villages of the south-western counties of England and dispatch them to Manchester.

The first industrial power to have large-scale recourse to migrant labour from another country was also Britain. After the famine of 1845–7 hundreds of thousands of Irish peasants, their agriculture destroyed by English land policies, their families dispersed and decimated by starvation, crossed the sea to Liverpool and Glasgow. In their new situation they were without a trade. They had to accept low wages. They were mobile. They were dis-organized. They were seen by the English working class as inferiors, and were accused by them of cutting wages. They lived in the worst slums, which became Irish ghettos. They worked as navvies, dockers, steel-workers, and they were indispensable to the building of the physical installations necessary for the expansion of British industry after the invention of the steam engine.

TWENTIETH-CENTURY ROAD GANG OF MIGRANT WORKERS, SWITZERLAND

NINETEENTH-CENTURY RAILWAY NAVVIES IN ENGLAND, MANY OF WHOM WERE IRISH IMMIGRANTS

The migration of workers in Europe today is in one respect different. The majority are prevented or discouraged from settling permanently in the country in which they work. Governments and multi-national corporations plan their policies on a global scale, and the advantages for capitalism of worker migration being temporary are considerable.

He is not aware of his historical antecedents. And the convenience for capitalism of his migration being temporary accords with his own wishes. He certainly did not come with the intention of staying. Of those who later decide that their survival will be surer if they stay and who are able to settle permanently (the largest national group among these are Italians who, because Italy is a member of the European Economic Community, have residential rights) – of these the majority remain uncertain about their decision. It became too late to return home, he explains and lifts up his arms in a gesture of protest-become-resignation, what could I do?

If he is aware of a current, a tide which is stronger than his own volition, he thinks of it, in an undifferentiated way, as Life. This view of the wholeness and inexplicability of what happens to him upholds a sense of destiny and proposes a special endurance and courage. This is not to say he will never resist, that he will accept every injustice. It is to say that tragedy is more real to him than explanations. Yet the history which he neither knows nor seeks to know is there: it is part of his situation, it belongs already to his experience. It is part of his tragedy.

The naturalness of his inferior status – the naturalness with which he is accorded his inferiority by people, by institutions, by the everyday etiquette of the metropolis, by ready-made phrases and arguments – would never be so complete and unhesitating if his function, and the inferior status which it entailed, were new.

He has been here from the beginning.

They come here, what do they come for?

To get as much money as they can and send it out of the country. They are not interested in anything. Just money. It's always the same story. They take our money, they take our jobs, they take our houses – if they could, if we let them, they would take over everything.

Do you know they all eat out of the same plate? They are barbarians.

They try to bring their families in. They take over whole streets and live twenty to a house. They say we exploit them, but the landlord is usually one of them. They do business amongst themselves, their own business.

Do you know what they are used to where they come from? Backstreets are like palaces to them. They don't know how to live in a modern city. It'll take them a hundred years to catch up.

A migrant worker: You could call us the niggers of Europe.

All of them carry knives. No woman is safe.

They live in those barracks like animals.

They certainly do business among themselves.

The piece only goes half way in. It jams. He has been shown not to put his hand behind it. A red light goes on. It is like a tree that has fallen across a stream, the water frothing on one side. Only here he has no idea of what has happened. The stoppage is as mysterious as the speed. He wrenches with his hand, glances round; then he has a compulsion to shut his eyes. He remembers his cousin saying: If a tree falls in a forest, the other trees hold it up, that's why I am staying here and not going to the abroad. The machine has stopped and its parts are as inert as a buried wheel. He had inserted the piece the wrong way up. The foreman insults him for his mistake.

Migrants are widely termed Zigeuner (gypsy), Lumpenpack (rag-pack), Kameltreiber (camel-rider), Zitronen-schüttler (lemon-squeezer), or Schlangenfresser (snake-eater).

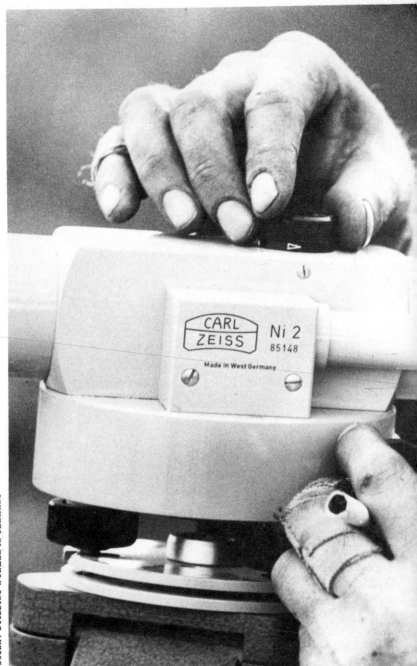

116

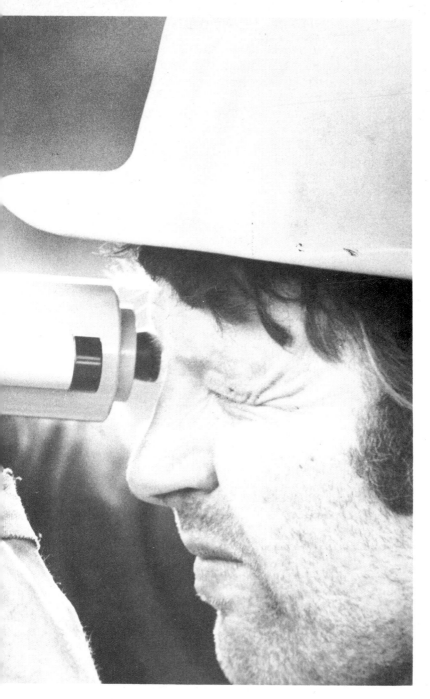

Outwardly he accepts this. Inwardly he calls upon his pride to remind himself who he is and what he has already achieved. The greatest of his achievements is that he is working here.

What do they come for? The simple argument is as follows. Since the war, and particularly during the last fifteen years, the economy of Western Europe has been expanding faster than the population. This produced a labour shortage. In the Mediterranean countries, by contrast, there is a problem of 'over-population' because modern medicine, originating in the developed countries, is reducing infant mortality and disease everywhere. What happened therefore was that men without work began to come to where there was work: work which, on the whole, and certainly by their standards, was well paid.

No statement in this argument is untrue. Yet it disguises the truth. How opaque the disguise of words.

When he crossed the frontier every word spoken or written was meaningless to him. At first he tried to guess what words meant. Most of the words addressed to him were instructions or orders. If he guessed wrong he was in trouble. So he learnt it was safer not to guess. He treated the sounds of the unknown language as if they were silence.

To break through his silence.

He learnt twenty words of the new language. But, to his amazement at first, their meaning changed when he spoke them. He asked for coffee. What the word coffee signified to the barman was that he was asking for coffee in a bar where he should not be asking for coffee. He learnt girl. What the word girl meant, when he used it, was that he was a randy dog.

Is it possible to see through the opaqueness of the words?

The labour shortage in Western Europe is not the result of under-population. It is a specific shortage in a specific system of production. There are not enough workers willing, at the wages offered, to do the low-paid manual jobs.

Modern technology has increased the productivity of labour. The proportion of workers directly engaged in production has therefore been reduced. But to maintain high productivity and to sell its products a vastly increased labour force has been needed for servicing, planning, controlling and marketing activities. More jobs now involve the social processing of commodities and consumers than the processing of raw materials.

Some of these are integrally related to the new technology – scientists, researchers, engineers, technicians, highly skilled maintenance and repair men, etc. – but many more (both absolutely and relatively) are concerned in one way or another with the manipulation and absorption of the surplus made possible by the increased productivity of the underlying production workers. Under this heading one could list government workers of all kinds, including teachers; those employed in the many branches of the sales apparatus, including most of the personnel of the mass-communications media; workers and salaried personnel in finance, insurance, and real estate; and the providers of many different kinds of personal service from beauty treatment to sports spectacles.

The work involved in the new range of jobs is often frustrating and dehumanized. But it is not physically arduous, and the conventional values of society, re-imposed every day by the media, confer an enviable social status upon the new jobs. The white collar offers membership of a higher division of labour. Higher because less physical. Higher because more abstracted. Higher because of the 'sophistication' of the equipment used.

This new category of work has altered the quality of remuneration expected for work in general. Remuneration now includes a life-style which, as it were, houses the wage even while being dependent on it. Parallel to this, the trade unions, whose bargaining power increased during the post-war period of economic expansion, were able to win higher wages for many of the skilled workers still directly involved in production. These higher wages were not cut from profits but came from the extra surplus created by increased productivity. Profits increased more than wages.

Nevertheless, essential unskilled work had by no means been eliminated. And the expansion of the economy required more of this unskilled labour.

Who was to build the new buildings and motorways, make the castings, clean the cities, man the assembly lines, quarry the minerals, load the goods, bury the pipe lines?

MIGRANT WORKERS SHOPPING FOR WEEKEND, STUTTGART, GERMANY

A 'utopian' solution might have existed in theory: to attract to these essential jobs some of the inactive or unproductive sections of the population (young men not yet working, women at home, some of the supernumeraries in the unproductive sector) by paying exceedingly high wages and by improving working conditions beyond recognition. But to do this would not only have cut into profits, not only overthrown the wage structure of the entire economy – far worse, it would have contradicted the central ethical law of the system: the principle of a hierarchic society based on the division of labour between mind and hand, spiritual and manual, high and low.

In any case there was no need for anything utopian. An unemployed labour force existed. It existed in a state of under-development, created by the development of those countries now suffering a labour shortage.

Next week when he makes the same mistake, he receives a minor injury to his hand. He stares at his blood.

The accident rate in France for industrial migrant workers is eight times higher than that for indigenous workers.

There are a number of reasons for immigrant workers' high accident rates:

1. Most immigrant workers are of rural origin and are unfamiliar with industrial work.
2. As most accidents happen during periods of training and adjustment to a specific job, immigrants who have only recently arrived to work in industry in a Western European country, and who change jobs more frequently than indigenous workers, are more often in this situation.
3. Language difficulties are a frequent cause of accidents, many of which occur because people cannot read warning signs or understand warning shouts from workmates.
4. Immigrant workers are over-represented in industries and types of work where the accident risk is highest.
5. Immigrants work very long hours. It is a well-known fact that most industrial accidents happen at the end of the working day, when fatigue reduces attentiveness.

The terms of the equation should by now be clear.

In the cities of his country, poverty and a blocked economy have led to a proliferation of the unproductive service sector. Every day more peasants abandon the countryside and move to the nearest city to look for a living; their main hope there is to invent a service to sell – to try to become a shoe-black, an unofficial parking attendant, a match-seller, a man with a weighing machine. The proliferation leads to starvation and physical chaos. The chaos is exemplified in the shanty-town. This is what he left.

He left his country to come to the metropolis. In the metropolis the concentration of capital and the affluence of goods

have led to the proliferation of another kind of unproductive service sector, made up of salaried employees whose principal function is to produce and reproduce the consumer. The metropolitan proliferation leads to wastage and environmental chaos. The focal point of its apparatus is the shop window as a magnifying lens.

129

To a man from a village the fact that people live in the same place is primary. He is living now in a city in which he is the witness of luxury. Some of it shocks him, some of it impresses him. But the sight of it, the fact that he is a witness of it, entails a promise: a promise addressed to him by simple virtue of his being there.

Between the wastes of poverty and the wastes of affluence, he works. He works to save enough money to change his life. To benefit from the promise.

Meanwhile, in his country of origin, the conditions which create rival unemployment persist.

Between the two wastes he works.

At home he worked in a small-town abattoir two days a week. It was an event in that town – something to be discussed several days in advance – if more than ten animals were to be slaughtered at a time. The abattoir was a low building, its area no larger than a threshing floor. Half the week there was no one there, no animals in the pen behind it, its doors padlocked. It stood where the hills began, by the side of a gravel quarry. In a corner of the quarry there was a rust-stained gulley where the drain from the abattoir ran out. Where he works now, eighty cattle are slaughtered in an hour: 150,000 a year.

When he was taken on, he considered himself doubly fortunate. He had found work and he would learn more of the trade. At home one man held the sheep and the other stabbed it at the back of the neck. The sheep stopped struggling but did not lose consciousness until one of them stuck it so that it bled. All this on the floor. Then both the men, bent over the animal together, would dress and skin and eviscerate it, talking while they did so or working silently and taking a pride in their deftness with the knife. In the winter when it was cold, the carcass gave off a warmth.

Whether it was an oxen that had to be tied with a rope to a ring on the floor and stunned with a hammer, or a sheep that could be held, whether he was working kneeling on the floor or at the table, whether the owner of the animal was there or not, he thought of what he was doing in terms of meat to be bought and eaten. The better he worked, the less would be wasted. And he worked very slowly, for there was no reason to work fast unless it was at the end of a hot day.

In the full summer heat blood smells different – producing a kind of urgency through a fear of nausea: a fear so improbable that it is the more striking.

In the city the scale of the abattoir astounded him. And the speed of the line. The only clearing of relative stillness is around the bleeding trough where the cattle, having been stunned and automatically hoisted, hang like tree trunks from which red streams flow with a leisure which, although mortal, seems natural. After ten long minutes the neck pouches are opened and the rhythm of the machines takes over. The bled forest opens on to a highway.

He worked on the highway. The head is severed. The food pipe is tied up to avoid contamination. The first foreleg is skinned and removed: the animal is transferred to another hoist and the second leg (from which previously the body hung) is then removed. His job (unskilled) was to wash the heads after they had been scalped and to push the hoof truck, when it was full, to the work rooms off the main floor. A truck full of hoofs: the broken experience of a hundred fields.

The hind legs are spread and the carcass moves on rollers past the dressers, rippers and skinners. Hydraulic hide-pullers grip the open edge of the belly and pull the hide backwards across the sides. The hide is removed from the back.

His other job, if he found himself without work, was to help three other men like himself taking the hides to the hide room. The hides steamed and were wet as if after a cloud-burst following lightning which had killed the herd and packed them together with thunder.

An electric blade sawed the breast bone. From the open chest the red and green offal is taken, inspected, dispatched. The social division of the carcass begins. The meat that will be eaten by, among others, migrant workers, in barracks and lodging rooms, is separated here from meat to be eaten in restaurants and houses by the rich and salaried.

The different parts go to different butchers in different districts. There are streets of fillet steak and roast beef, and streets of the skirt and intestines. This social distribution of the viscera and parts is as efficient as the saw which, operated from a platform coming down on to the carcass, now splits it into two sides. Quickly it ascends, the saw-operator, like St Peter returning into the sky.

For the well-fed who work with their brains: the best muscles of the animal from the backbone to the rump. For the unskilled manual workers: head trimmings, heart, stomach, lungs, spleen, udder, shins and tail.

St Peter splits a carcass every forty seconds. In sixty minutes half a ton of ox liver has been taken. The heap of livers looks like one enormous liver.

He asked himself whether his town, if its abattoir were better equipped, could not serve all the towns in the province. The problem would be refrigeration. Here the lorries were refrigerated.

A worker one day threatened to shut him in a cooler. He did not understand the words the man was bellowing, but it turned out to be a joke. Several local workers were not unfriendly to him. After a few days there was one who made a sign that he should come and eat with a group of them. Every day they went to a near-by restaurant to eat meat ferociously. They had an enormous appetite for meat. He went with them, but the meal cost more than he wanted to spend, and he was unused to eating so much. Most days he ate a sandwich by himself in a bar and drank two strong black coffees.

As the days passed and the flow of heads to be washed and hoofs to be shifted never ceased, he began to have the impression that the machines were multiplying the animals: that they took one and turned it into a hundred. This impression did not disturb him and it never lasted for more than an instant. Indeed it was only sustained as an impression because the brief instants repeated themselves: the duration of a single instant would have escaped his notice.

The hardest part of the day was the evening after work. He slept in a large cellar in a lodging house with fifteen other men of different nationalities, many of them only staying there a few nights. Between working and sleeping he spent his time walking through the streets and occasionally going into a café.

He would think: At this hour everybody with the horses, donkeys, cows, goats, sheep, insects, hens, cats, dogs, was fast asleep. Only he was awake walking in the unheard-of street.

No matter how limited a man's field of vision, his imagination knows no bounds. A man who has never been outside his village . . . can still create a whole imaginary world that may reach as far as the stars. Without travelling, a man can penetrate to the other end of the world.

On these walks he became more and more conscious that there were no animals to be seen. Sometimes he passed a dog on a lead, or a cat ran close to the wall. This unfamiliar lack of animals distressed him. He wondered whether they might not exist and be mysteriously hidden. Then he wondered whether they were there in the streets and waste lots he was crossing, but invisibly so.

He walked back to the abattoir, crossed the railway lines and approached the hunger pens where tomorrow's cattle were kept, without fodder but with water. The nightwatchman shone a torch in his face and asked him what he was doing. He said he worked there and was taking a walk. He said this in his language. The nightwatchman shooed him away, but not violently, because he feared that the foreigner might carry a knife. He shooed him away, half laughing, saying he should go to bed.

A few days later he asked if he could change his job. He would prefer, he said, to be hosing the cattle down before they enter the stunning pen. He was told two men were doing that who had done it for ten years.

His two delusions (if it is required that they should be called that) began to reinforce one another. The machines were multiplying the carcasses. The meat would never be eaten. The heads he was washing were the same ones as he washed yesterday. During the night they re-joined the necks from which they had been severed and re-grew their skin. The hoofs grew again on the cannons of the legs. The sides came together and the hides were unripped and whole again. He knew this because he recognized each morning the same eyes in the scalped heads. Meanwhile along the streets and between the buildings an invisible herd grazed each night. He never visited the hunger pens again.

He was not the victim of these delusions. He spoke of them to nobody. They did not interfere with his work. He did not believe in them. They were simply the form which, from time to time, his unease took upon itself. This unease became more pressing.

After a month he had enough money to pay for his return railway journey. But instead, he hid in one of the cattle vans going south.

When questioned by his family – he was unmarried – about why he had returned so soon and about how he would find the money to pay back what he had borrowed to go in the first place, he shook his head: Even if I don't find work here nobody is going to put me out into the street. There it could happen any moment, he explained.

Why do they come here? For the money. And they send it out of the country. That's why prices go up.

A migrant worker: If you want to earn the same as us, you have only to do the same jobs as us.

In dreams separate, even contradictory, truths can be entwined. A thing may be two things at the same time. A table of food and a sledge. A hook and a beak.

Every time he goes to work he is the subject of three calculations: two are being made by others, and one is his own.

First Calculation

For capitalism migrant workers fill a labour shortage in a specially convenient way. They accept the wages offered and, in doing so, slow down wage-increases in general. The significance of this is explained in a Report by the German Institute for Economic Research:

'Although opposition to the continual inflow of foreign workers is to be found here and there, it is necessary to realize that with a labour market cut off from other countries the pressure of wages in the Federal Republic would become considerably stronger, due to increased competition by employers for the domestic labour potential. This increased pressure of costs could hardly fail to affect the competitiveness of West German enterprises, both in the export markets and at home.'

Capitalism requires an ever-increasing accumulation of capital. This demands ever-increasing productivity. But the market does not always respond in regular correspondence with production: hence the cycles of recession and expansion and a rising tendency to inflation. Since the war these have been controlled, but controlling them involves fluctuations creating unemployment. There must be a labour reserve, which can be laid off during recessions and brought in when the economy is expanding. If the organized national working class formed this entire labour reserve and suffered accordingly, they might begin to demand that an end be put to the system: they might become a revolutionary proletariat. If, however, a large part of the labour reserve is made up of migrant workers, they can be 'imported' when needed and 'exported' (sent home) when made temporarily redundant, and there need be no political repercussions, for the migrants have no political rights and little political influence.

The migrant is in several other ways an 'ideal' worker. He is eager to work overtime. He is willing to do shift work at night. He arrives politically innocent – that is to say without any proletarian experience. Those who apply for work at Citröen are often asked to show their tickets to prove that they have just arrived in France.

Any individual migrant who does become a leader or 'militant' can be immediately and easily expelled from the country. The trade unions are unlikely to defend him. Migrants pay taxes and social security contributions but will not draw many benefits during their temporary residence. Their cost to the system in terms of social capital can be kept to a minimum. It is made difficult for a migrant's family to join him: hence his children don't have to be educated: as a 'single' man (a man made single) he will not greatly exacerbate the working-class housing shortage. By German law a migrant must have a living/sleeping space of six square metres. 70 per cent of migrant workers in Germany live singly, using not much more than that guaranteed minimum space. It is true that he may send a third of his wages out of the country but, as has already been pointed out, a large proportion of the money sent away is spent on goods manufactured in the country where he works. Inter-governmental agreements about the reception of migrants often involve trade agreements in the obverse direction.

Then there is a global convenience. The employment of migrant workers relieves unemployment in their countries of origin. If all the eleven million migrants now in north-western Europe returned home, their presence at home could well lead to explosive political situations; the most interested imperialist country would then be forced to intervene in order to preserve 'law and order'. A Spanish migrant worker: 'If we started a large-scale social revolution today in Spain, we would have to reckon with possible American intervention tomorrow. The countries of origin (where we come from) are becoming increasingly more dependent.' With many workers abroad part of the calculation is that social revolution in their countries of origin is less likely.

Most important of all, however, is the political part of the calculation. Migrant workers do the most menial jobs. Their chances of promotion are exceedingly poor. When they work in gangs, it is arranged that they work together with other foreigners. Equal working relationships to indigenous workers are kept to a minimum. The migrant workers have a different language, a different culture and different short-term interests. They are immediately identifiable – not as individuals, but as a group (or a series of national groups). As a group they are at the bottom of every scale: wages, type of work, job security, housing, education, purchasing power.

Thus indigenous workers see another group, less privileged than they are, who differ from them. A Marxist would immediately point out that their differences are secondary, and that they share the same class interest. The recognition of this truth is necessary for any revolutionary movement. But the political convenience of migrant labour for capitalism lies precisely in the fact that this theoretical truth is overlaid daily and disguised by experience.

The indigenous worker sees the migrant in an 'inferior' position, and what he sees and hears emphasizes how the migrant is different. Different to the point of being unknowable. Imperceptibly – there is no moment of decision – the two characteristics fuse. From being unknowable the migrant comes to be seen as being beneath understanding: as being intrinsically unpredictable, disorganized, feckless, devious. And then the inverted commas around inferior disappear: what has become the migrant's intrinsic inferiority is now expressed in his inferior status. What he is paid to do reflects what he is. The fusion has occurred.

Such a view, widespread in the indigenous working class, can in certain circumstances lead to overt and violent racism. An acute housing shortage or any other form of urban frustration can spark off riots or systematic racial persecution. When this happens it is not particularly convenient for the ruling class. They will call it a regrettable excess. The convenience for them is less dramatic and more lasting.

The presence of migrant workers, seen as intrinsically inferior and therefore occupying an inferior position in society, confirms the principle that a social hierarchy – of some kind or another – is justified and inevitable. The working class comes to accept the basic bourgeois claim that social inequality is finally an expression of natural inequality.*

Once accepted, the principle of natural inequality gives rise to a fear: the fear of being cheated out of one's natural and rightful place in the hierarchy. The threat is thought of as coming from both above and below. The working class will become no less suspicious of the bosses. But they may become equally jealous of their privileges over those they consider to be their natural inferiors.

Certain political theorists will now say: Yes, yes, the old tactic of Divide and Rule; the working class must answer: United We Stand! Divided We Fall! It is more subtle than that. We are in a labyrinth.

---

* The famous bourgeois demand for Equality with which the bourgeoisie first challenged feudalism and absolutism was a demand for artificial inequalities to be abolished, so that nature should be allowed to work freely according to its own laws. Natural inequality in the place of artificial inequality.

The principle of natural inequality rests upon judging men and women according to their abilities. It is obvious that ability varies, and that abilities are unequally distributed. It can even be admitted that in a certain field an inferior can show himself to be superior, eg, a Greek may be a better dancer than a German: a Spaniard a better guitarist than a Dutchman. What determines a person's position in the social hierarchy is the sum of his abilities as required in that particular social and economic system. He is no longer seen as another man, as the unique centre of his own experience: he is seen as the mere conglomerate of certain capacities and needs. He is seen, in other words, as a complex of functions within a social system. And he can never be seen as more than that unless the notion of equality between men is re-introduced.

Equality has nothing to do with capacity or function: it is the recognition of being. The Church arranged earth and heaven hierarchically. But to make the idea of the soul convincing it had to concede that all men were equal before God. Karamazov went further: if all are not saved, what good is the salvation of one only?

Only in relation to what men are in their entirety can a social system be judged just or unjust: otherwise it can be merely assessed as relatively efficient or inefficient. The principle of equality is the revolutionary principle, not only because it challenges hierarchies, but because it asserts that all men are equally whole. And the converse is just as true: to accept inequality as natural is to become fragmented, is to see oneself as no more than the sum of a set of capacities and needs.

This is why the working class, if it accepts the natural inferiority of the migrants, is likely to reduce its own demands to economic ones, to fragment itself and to lose its own political identity. When the indigenous worker accepts inequality as the principle to sustain his own self-esteem, he reinforces and completes the fragmentation which society is already imposing upon him.

That this will continue happening is the calculation of the ruling class.

SABA pro FP 32 telecomputer

Schwarzweiß-Portable mit
44-cm-Bild. Minimale Wärme-
entwicklung durch voll-
transistoriertes Niedervolt-
Chassis. Programmanzeige
durch 6 Leuchtdioden.

Bildröhren-Schnellschaltung.
Hochwirksame Antennen?.
Drei attraktive Farbvarianten.

143

Second Calculation

Most migrant workers are not politically conscious of their exploitation. Their thought is traditional – either Catholic or Muslim; their expectation of change, their humanism, is gathered into hopes of individual and family achievement. It is too soon to know how they might become politicized if they stayed longer. The employers, aware of the inconvenience of a politically conscious sub-proletariat, plan for a continual 'rotation' of foreign labour so that no workers will stay too long.

A very small number of migrant workers do think politically. Sometimes this is the result of their experience of oppression in their own countries; sometimes the result of their disillusion, their clarity, about what they see in the metropolitan countries. A migrant's experience of capitalism, because he is exploited in every field, becomes, if he is politically aware of it at all, a very unified experience. In his life he is brought face to face, always negatively, with the unity of the entire system. The steps of his thought become correspondingly large: far larger than those of theorists within the system. Thus a few migrant workers, a handful, become revolutionaries. Their position is highly vulnerable because they can always be deported within twenty-four hours. Their position is potentially influential because they speak the same language, live the same lives, as the mass of their politically unconscious compatriots.

This is the situation in which the second calculation is made: that of the official trade unions.

All the trade unions in the metropolitan countries once opposed the use of immigrant labour. They feared it as a weapon (he has not thought of himself as a minute part of a weapon) to be used by the employers to keep wages down. Despite the opposition of the unions, immigrant labour was increasingly brought in. This forced the unions to change their policy and to try to attract the foreign workers as members.

Migrants have the right to join existing trade unions. In France and Switzerland they may not hold an official union post. In every country they are barred from political activity – what constitutes political activity being left to the discretion of the authorities. In Germany about 30 per cent of migrant workers are unionized; in France and Switzerland about 10 per cent. The majority of migrants, whether they belong to a union or not, are sceptical about the unions being willing or able to fight for their interests.

In fact, the unions have not resolved their original dilemma. (There is no reason why their policy about immigrant workers should be more global or radical than the narrow reformism of their general policies.) They proclaim that the working class is international. They demand equal pay for equal work, and in most countries this is the law – although it can fairly easily be got round because migrants are often not aware of their rights or, if they are without papers, have no rights. Certain unions publish papers in the language of the principal migrant groups. On occasions the unions support strike action by migrants. (The unions' fear that migrants would act as scab labour proved wrong; they have nearly always followed official strikes.) The unions appeal for improved living conditions for migrants. But they have never been able to think or act beyond the proposition that the migrant worker belongs to the country he has left and therefore does not belong where he works. This has made the unions power-less before the contradictory facts which underpin the proposition. It needs to be called a proposition (although it is accepted by both indigenous and migrant workers) because the word belong, is, in the context, a mystification.

Some of the contradictory facts are as follows:

The migrant knows he is here on sufferance so all his spontaneous interests are short-term ones.	The migrant takes the jobs nobody else will.
	The migrant cannot get promotion.
	The migrant is the first to be made redundant.
The migrant wants to earn as quickly as possible. So he is inclined to work overtime, exceed production norms on piece work, take, if possible, a second part-time job.	The migrant is always liable to victimization.
	The migrant is divided from other migrants and from indigenous workers by a language barrier.
Many migrants have, illegally, resorted to private deals with their employers.	The migrant performs many of the most dangerous jobs and has fewer insurance benefits.
	The migrant has no proper life, only work: no proper living conditions, only working conditions.
Migrants tend to mistrust all officials and all organizations.	
This may threaten the bargaining power of the indigenous working class.	This means that migrant workers are the most exploited of all.

The only possible way beyond these contradictions, would be for the trade unions to contest the migrant's inferior status by demanding right of promotion, right of political activity, right of residence for as long as he wishes, right of entry for his family. Yet to make these demands would be to alienate the majority of union members who have accepted their natural superiority over the migrant. It would also involve the unions in a head-on confrontation with government and management, who argue that the national economic interest – which includes the interest of the national working class – depends upon immigrant labour being used exactly as it is.

In practice the trade-union leadership does not make these demands. Its calculation is otherwise. That the trade unions can keep the exploitation of the migrants within such limits that the living standard of the national working class is not affected, and that, should extremist elements arise among the foreigners, the union apparatus will be able to isolate them.

Third Calculation

That he will save enough soon enough.

That his woman remains faithful to him.

That in the meantime he can arrange that some of his family join him.

That when once he has set himself up at home, he will never have to return here.

That his health holds out.

It is absurd to consider the health of migrant workers as though they were healthy or sick like others. Their function, the conditions of their presence here, are incompatible with the norms of preventive and clinical medicine. The norms do not apply to them. In France surveys have shown that the rate of mental illness among immigrants is two or three times higher than among French citizens. But the category of mental illness is suspect. It would be more, not less, scientific to say that immigrants suffer twice or three times as much from insecurity and unhappiness.

HOUSING FOR MIGRANTS, MOSTLY SINGLE, NEAR STUTTGART, GERMANY

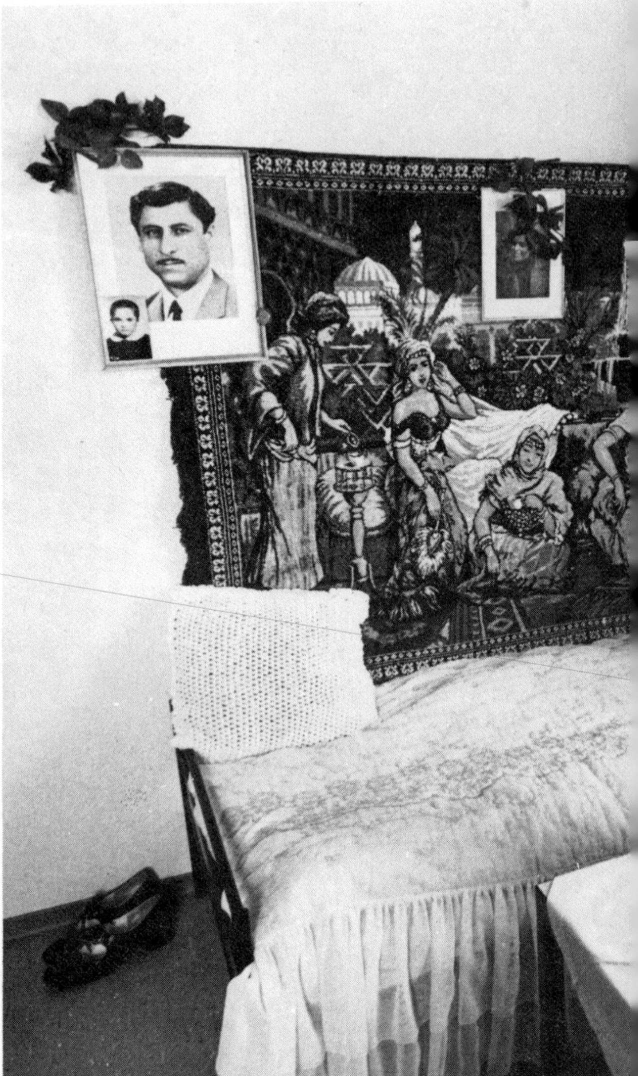

TURKISH WOMAN MIGRANT WORKER IN LODGING, GERMANY

A Report from under Geneva

Geneva today (1974) is a town of 250,000 inhabitants. Its population fifteen years ago was 195,000. Geneva is not an industrial centre: it is a centre of paper work, of contracts, deals, plans, treaties, agreements, reports. Most of these emanate from organizations dedicated in one way or another to international cooperation and exchange. The United Nations. The International Red Cross. The International Labour Office. Etc. Besides the governmental international agencies, there are also many multinational companies and banks. Geneva – perhaps more exclusively than any other town in Europe – is a capital of words: words written in reports and on cheques: spoken words, interpreted and recorded. All of them relate to what is happening in the rest of the world; and many of them go out into the world as recommendations. During the last fifteen years the number of words has much increased and, correspondingly, the town has grown.

This is particularly evident to the north in the area around the original League of Nations building and the new airport. Here new offices, new flats for their employees, new shops, new hotels for delegates, new roads and new parking-lots have extended far into what, fifteen years ago, were woods and fields. At that time the rain and snow which fell soaked into the earth. Today, in the new built-up area, the gutter water has to be run away. The existing drains and catchments for the north of the town are already overworked. The Town and Canton of Geneva therefore instructed their engineering department to work out a plan.

The plan was ambitious and progressive. It foresaw continuing growth: it considered the question of pollution: it resisted the temptation of a merely ad hoc and temporary solution and it was not timid about investing the taxpayers' money. The estimated cost of the new plan was £5 million. (It will cost far more.) It proposed a drainage system which would serve, not only the new suburbs, but all that part of Geneva which lies on the right bank of the lake.

To install drainage at street level would have seriously dislocated traffic – local and international – over a period of years. It would also have rendered new building more difficult – by over-crowding the network of pipes and services just below the surface. So the plan envisaged tunnelling thirty or more metres underground.

One tunnel was to run for five kilometres under the town and would collect all the rain and gutter water of the right bank and discharge it into the Rhone below the lake. A second tunnel was to run parallel with the first for more than half the way, and would carry electricity and telephone cables and water mains for the new buildings and the new offices in which so many plans on a world-scale were being drawn up. The diameter of each tunnel was to be 3.6 metres.

Tunnelling began in June 1971 and will continue until 1976. In tunnelling space restricts the amount of labour that can be used. Even with three faces being worked simultaneously, there is work for only a hundred men. Most of the men now working are Yugoslavs. There are also Spaniards and some Italians from South Italy. On the many building sites in Geneva most workers are migrants. In the tunnels they are 100 per cent migrant. The two engineers and one of the foremen are German.

The workers, except for a specialist mechanic and electrician, are on nine-month contracts. When the contract finishes they return to their Bosnian or Andalusian or Calabrian villages and then re-apply for another year's chance of tunnelling under the international metropolis. According to Swiss law the residence-permits (Type A) of these workers do not permit them to stay longer than 9 months (although they may continue to come year after year) nor to bring with them any of their family. While working in Geneva, they live in a wooden barracks belonging to the Swiss private contractors who are building the tunnel.

The plan, relying on the advice of geologists, assumed that nearly all the tunnelling would be through sandstone. For the planners of tunnels sandstone is ideal because it is rock not clay, yet it is not a hard rock: consequently there is no need for digging (as with clay) or blasting (as with hard rock) and, instead, a rotary cutting machine, 'a mechanical mole' can bore through the sandstone (at the rate of about 10 metres a shift) and leave the tunnel behind it.

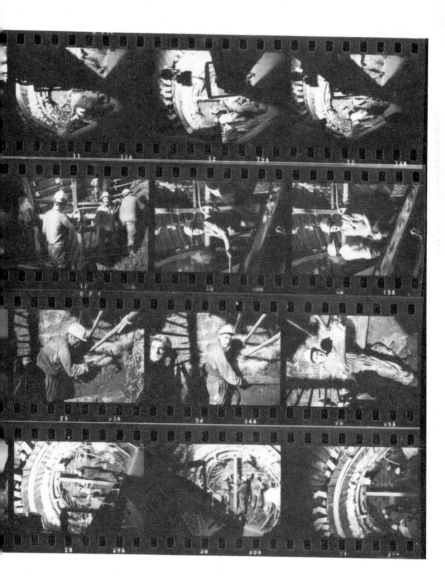

Unfortunately the geologists in Geneva were wrong in their predictions and the tunnels have run into wet earth and shingle. Here only shovels and hand-held pneumatic drills can be used, and after each advance of ten metres – which may now take a whole week – tubes are rammed fourteen metres into the face and solidifying chemicals injected to hold the water back. If the water breaks through, it can come at the rate of 120 litres per minute.

These two sets of conditions offer the underground worker a choice. He can work with the machine in the dry: or with the drills in the wet. Working with the machine is more unhealthy because of the very high dust content in the air. Masks are available but the strenuousness of the work means that wearing them – with a reduced oxygen intake – makes the heart race. Nobody, except sometimes the sitting driver of the machine, wears one. The dust carries with it the risk of silicosis. Silicosis is often cited as a common occupational disease afflicting coal miners. It is caused by fine particles of silica which have been breathed into the lungs remaining there and causing nodular lesions along the lymphatics and in the lung tissue. Two years' exposure to the dust particles can be enough to provoke the disease. Once it has begun there is no cure, and it can lead to total disability through the poorer and poorer functioning of the lungs. In coal itself there is no silica, but it is often present in the rock between seams. Sandstone – such as they are tunnelling through under Geneva – may consist of as much as 90 per cent silica.

Working in the wet is higher paid because it is more immediately uncomfortable and because the drilling and mucking out by hand requires considerable endurance.

The workers are divided into gangs of seven or eight. They are never all of the same nationality. Whereas the town above specializes in international interpreting, the members of a gang have scarcely a dozen words between them. Misunderstandings have led to accidents. On the other hand – benefiting output – work proceeds with little talk. Except for one crane-driver, none of the work is highly skilled and is fairly interchangeable; it involves mucking out earth and rocks at the face, keeping the conveyor belt clear, drilling when necessary, driving the train of trams between the face and the pit bottom, fitting the iron sections and grills which brace and line the inside of the tunnel, hosing liquid cement on to the grills, shovelling up, carting, and driving the machine. Each gang works an eight-hour shift, and three shifts work round the clock.

A gang is paid for nine hours, including a one-hour meal break. But nobody wants to eat in the tunnel. The air is stale. (Neither the water pumps nor the ventilating system work properly, but they are patched up when the word comes round that there is going to be an official inspection.) If the mole is drilling, a grey powder, fine as talc, lines skin, hair, nostrils, throat, lungs. The alternative of walking back to pit bottom and climbing up the ladders to the surface would take too much time and effort. So the gangs work eight hours without a serious stop. Anyway they have an interest in forcing the pace.

At the wages offered, indigenous labour refuses this work. Migrants undertake it in order to earn and save the maximum amount of money in the shortest time. Officially bonuses for extra output are illegal. Yet there are ways round this. And so the interests of migrant and contractor are made – apparently – to coincide. The faster a man works, or the worse the conditions so that he is entitled to a small compensatory supplement, the more he can save. For the contractor, the quicker the job is done, the greater the profit margin. An underground worker in the tunnels can earn between £300 and £350 per month.

About a quarter of his wages goes in tax, social security, and trade-union dues. (80 per cent of the men belong to the union.) If he lives austerely, he can still save or send home £150 a month. With these savings he imagines he is transforming his own life and his family's. Working in the tunnel, each man is more or less locked in his personal vision of a different future. This adds to the isolation caused by language. It can lead, some-times, to a kind of negligence – of the present and of the self.

Several aspects of the self are denied by the migrant's situation. He has no natural existence as a sexual being and no legitimate existence as a political being. He is there on sufferance for so long as he works in a tunnel.

At the beginning of 1973 four Spanish workers demanded better work conditions and went out on a half-day strike. By themselves. They were immediately sacked. Without a job they had no right to remain in the country. They were forced to return to Spain. Their record as undesirable 'extremists' was doubtless made known to the Spanish authorities. The Swiss trade union did nothing to protect them.

As a result of the Spaniards' action, however, a commission of four men, including a trade-union representative, came to inspect the tunnel working conditions. It declared them satisfactory.

During the remainder of the same year – with a work force which never exceeded one hundred – two workers were killed, a third had both his legs smashed (and was still in hospital months later), a fourth had his spine seriously damaged, a fifth lost his hearing because of an explosion, and there were numerous minor injuries.

The immediate causes of accidents are lack of space (for example between the trams and the sides of the tunnel there is no clearance on either side for a man), muck falling from un-protected conveyor-belts sometimes running at above head level, poor lighting, the difficulty of hearing due to the noise-level, problems of language, fatigue, impatient roofing in at the wet face, carelessness with machine controls.

Behind the immediate causes there is a general one. The only initiative still open to the migrant is the maximization of his earnings for the sake of a transformed future – or his attempt to transform his future. The contractors are concerned with the maximization of their profits. The relation between the two is exploitive. But, for very different reasons, both strive to reach the end of the tunnel as quickly as possible. For the migrant the alien present is expendable. (It is not only that the machines he uses were, at first, unfamiliar: compared with his previous life in the village, everything is alien.) For the contractor the migrant is expendable.

The barracks, in which the tunnel workers lodge, are owned by the contractors. Rent and food are deducted from wages

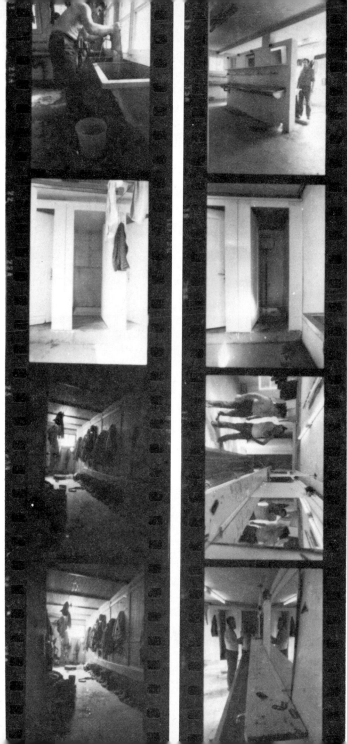

and marked on the pay-slips. The barracks are situated on the other side of the town from the main shaft. Each gang is transported to and from work in a minibus belonging to the firm. Transport is free.

After work, at the head of the shaft, there are cold-water washing facilities: for hot water the men await their return to the barracks. Geneva is a comparatively small town and the journey takes ten minutes.

In the main building of the barracks (housing approximately seventy men) there is a washroom with seven hot-water taps, seventeen cold-water taps, five lavatories and five showers (with hot water).

The men sleep four to a room. The room measures 4 metres by 5.5: walls and ceiling are wood. The heating is adequate

in winter. Apart from the cramped space, the principal inconvenience is noise: and this is exacerbated by the fact that each shift gets up and goes to bed at different hours. Voices and footsteps sound very loud even from the next room.

In situations in which time is served (conscripted service, prison) and which involves absence and sexual deprivation, to sleep is a deliverance from time. Sleeping becomes an active positive action.

Each occupant in a room has a bed, a small metal wardrobe (40 cm wide or alternatively half a wooden one; his locked suitcase on top of it), two small shelves, and the walls around, the ceiling above, his corner, to pin his pictures on.

The bed costs 50p a night (3.60 SF). The sheets are changed every two weeks. Except on Sundays, the rooms are tidied by three women (two Italians and one Yugoslav) who run the canteen and generally service the barracks.

There is a kitchen where men can prepare food themselves and eat it. Padlocked cupboards, like the wardrobes in the sleeping rooms, are supplied for keeping their food in.

There is also a canteen – large enough for a hundred men. Lunch costs 80p (5.70SF), breakfast (coffee and bread) 22p, supper 70p. In one corner there is a TV set. Scarcely any of the tunnel workers know enough French to follow the words. In the opposite corner there is a counter at which beer, wine, cigarettes, washing powder, razor blades are on sale.

For most men in the barracks, time off is time prolonged and wasted. They use the little they have to sleep in, wash their clothes, write letters. Nine out of ten are married. A few of the younger ones, who are willing to spend more money immediately, go into town on Sundays. For the majority their room with their bed in it is the centre of their leisure. Men from other rooms drop in to talk or listen. (During the silences they return home.) Often one of the four in the room has a portable gramophone. They put on records bought in the capital of their own province. Sometimes they sing or play cards. Much of the time, though sitting together, they withdraw into personal anticipations or memories.

No tunnel worker who has found that he has the
necessary endurance for the work, wishes to stop working in the
tunnel before he has fulfilled his savings target – which is likely to
take between three and five years. He knows that compared to many
of his compatriots he is well placed. Each year, after nine months'
work, he has to return to his country. Usually the contractor is
willing to re-employ him when he re-applies. But when he re-
enters Switzerland, he has to undergo a routine medical examination like all other migrants entering for the first or nth time. One of
his recurring fears is that the next time this happens, he will be
refused entry on the grounds of a shadow on his lung X-ray . . .

The only present reality for the migrant is work and the
fatigue which follows it. Leisure becomes alien to him because it
forces him to remember how far away he is from everything that he
still believes to be his real life. Beyond the present of work and his
own exertion, the rest of his life is reduced to a series of fixed images
relating to past and future, to his values and hopes. These images
are the landmarks of his life, but they remain static; they do not
develop. (The consequences of economic underdevelopment
permeate a whole life.) They cannot develop because they are
beyond the reach of his energy. Only by applying his energy to
work does he overcome the frustration of this, for he believes that
by saving his wages he will be able to rejoin these images and
animate them. As soon as he stops working, he is haunted by static
images. The images are static in themselves and yet they are
shifting in a terrible way. He has the impression that his own image
and those of his previous life are hurtling through space, like stars
travelling in different directions, so that the distance between them
is always increasing and becoming greater. From this impression
work is the only relief.

OLD WOMAN IN MARKET, GREECE

172

PEASANT GIRL WORKING IN FIELD

An Italian: During the day I have my work and my workmates. I think about what I can earn and work and work. I keep on telling myself that I am doing it for my family. But after work and on Sundays it is hellish.

How?

To ask directions in hell is difficult. If its topography were simple, men would walk out into the open countryside and lie on the banks of the wide river.

How?

Normally an awareness of a life's time is like a space around and yet within the person. Just as the measures of exterior time – hours, days, seasons, years - are dependent upon the solar system, so the self's time is constructed like a system rotating round a sun or a nucleus of self-consciousness. The felt space of a life's time may be represented by a circle.

The circle is filled at any given moment with past, present and future. The self cannot relate to a single point in time because it is predicated upon a continuity. I was, I am, I may be, is the minimum proposition of the word I when pronounced by itself. Within the circle the past exists in the form of buried and free-standing memories, the future in the form of fears and hopes; the present enters as it occurs and, immediately, the past and future relate to it. The three form an amalgam which is expressed in the intentionality of the person's actions at that moment. Such intentionality is informed by the past, it exists in the present, and it is directed towards a future. But for the amalgam to be formed, the elements constituting the past and future of his life's time need to be free and unfixed. A phobia, for example, might fix them, and make the victim of that phobia incapable of acting intentionally in relation to what was present.

Elements of past and future
free to form an amalgam with
the present.

Phobias apart, exterior circumstances can disturb the normal process. For example the suffering of loss. It happens in bereavement. A life has come to an end. For that life or towards it no more initiatives are possible. There is only the stillness of death. Perhaps the stillness suggests peace, but at first its fixity is terrible. And the fixity acts retrospectively. None of the life which is over can now be changed. The bereaved goes back to live again his part in that life. If he could re-live it as he originally lived it, he would be able to experience the still open possibilities of the life now ended. But when the bereaved return to the past, they can never entirely forget what has prompted their return : they go back to the past to foretell a death. The past is robbed of its future, which is now the present. To the extent that the bereaved wants to go on sharing the past life of the dead person, his own past becomes fixed. It is then as though the elements of the past line the circumference of the circle, and the future elements withdraw, losing all immediacy. I have nothing to live for now.

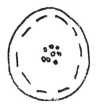

In bereavement the past
becomes fixed and
the future withdraws.

The past acts as a wall which prevents the present entering the life's time; or, if it filters in, it is transformed immediately into terms of the past. Everything he sees reminds him of what he can no longer see; and what he is reminded of becomes the essential experience, not what he sees. Supposing the period of bereavement passes. The future becomes available again, the present impinges, and they pull the past out of its fixity. The amalgam of intentionality is formed once more. The recovery is not the result of circumstances changing. The death is irreversible. It is the result of the life's time finally accepting the death and surrounding it, the loss becoming part of that life.

Loss is final. (At least at the level of our particular rationality, and this is not the moment to try to go further.) Absence can be thought of as temporary. Yet the suffering of enforced absence can destroy intentionality more thoroughly and for longer than bereavement. Imprisonment is the extreme example. The prisoner suffers the double pain of absence. He misses everything he feels as absent. At the same time, that which is absent, continues without him. He lacks and he is lacking. Yet absence is not final loss. His sentence has an end. He can envisage how he will rejoin the absent. This is a source of hope but it is also the pivot of the violence of imprisonment. Increasingly he may begin to live by way of memory and anticipation, until the two of them become indistinguishable, until he anticipates his release in the future as the moment when he will rejoin all that was left in the past. Imprisonment is designed as the categorical denial of the present. Prisoners may outwit the design by consciously putting the present of their sentence to their own use, by using it to transform themselves. (This is probably easier for prisoners of conscience or political prisoners because what led them to prison had more purpose.) If a prisoner is unable to do this, the past and future of his life's time may block out the present almost completely.

Imprisonment can cause past and future to lock together against the present.

Events occur, things happen, but they do not enter his life's time. He lives only the present of things exterior to him, not his own. If these things are near by, within the prison, he is said to be institutionalized. If they are too far away, he is said to have gone mad.

When he is released, he has to try to re-acquire the habit of admitting the present. But this present 'at liberty' may now confuse him, because it does not conform to his imagined image of it, based on the past. Life has continued in his absence, and he himself has changed. The second may be the more disconcerting. The changes in himself occurred during a present (his time inside) which he experienced as exterior to him; he does not understand the changes; he believes that something was done to him. (And he is right.) He tries to test himself and the world – to re-establish an instant unity between both on his terms: this can well mean another 'crime'. He becomes a recidivist: a man locked in his own static time – save when he breaks out for an instant. He has been made the product of an imprisonment which is now a life sentence, either in or out of the cells. The diagram (opposite), instead of remaining metaphorical, has become substantial and real.

Most nineteenth-century emigration was permanent. Sometimes the migrant maintained links with the family who had not accompanied him. But his departure was like a death. And after a period of bereavement both he and those he left behind thought of his presence in the distant new country as being another life.

Today the temporary migrant worker suffers a kind of imprisonment in a prison without frontiers.

In certain barracks the authorities have tried to forbid migrant workers keeping their suitcases in their sleeping rooms on the grounds that they make the room untidy. The workers have strongly resisted this, sometimes to the point of going on strike. In these suitcases they keep personal possessions, not the clothes they put in the wardrobes, not the photographs they pin to the wall, but articles which, for one reason or another, are their talismans. Each suitcase, locked or tied round with cord, is like a man's memory. They defend their right to keep the suitcases.

comment vivre en espagne

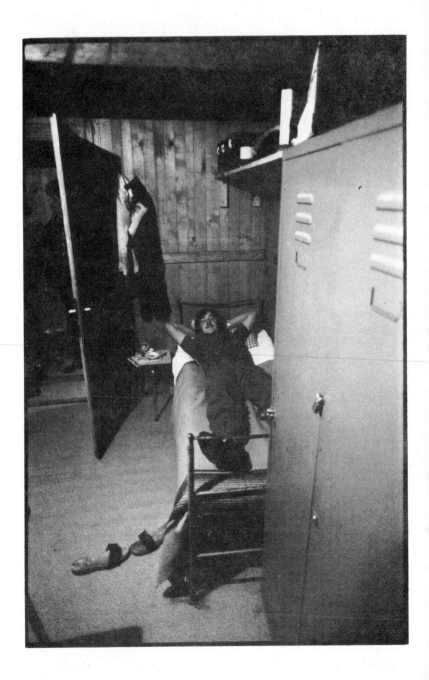

He is young and unmarried. He got up late, washed carefully, shaved and dressed. He put on only the clothes he had bought in the city: the nattily cut suit, the large tie the same colour as the shirt, the socks with zigzags, the cuff links in the form of golden wheels. He arranged the handkerchief in his breast pocket. Most Sundays he and two friends take the bus to the city centre. These outings are like rehearsals, preparing them for the performance. The performance will be when he will have a car, when he will drive back to the village, when he will be the man who knows the city like the back of his own hand, who no longer lives in a barracks but has a flat of his own, a resident's permit, a list of telephone numbers, and who will then have decided to marry a girl from his own country and to bring her back as his bride to the metropolis where, unlike his parents, he will have only two children, one son and one daughter. In the blotched mirror above the row of basins he arranges, for the second time, the handkerchief in his pocket.

While serving his time, the migrant worker faces two kinds of present. Work time, and 'time-off'.

The work time he is paid for. He collects units of it when he collects his wages. As time, as a present, it does not become his, joining with his past and future. In the work process itself his intentionality is reduced to a minimum. The timing of the job works him. But in exchange for his collection of units he will acquire opportunities in the future, and these will enter his life's time.

If one sees all his years of working abroad as a single act, it is an act of his own choice, containing intention. But within that act, the present of days, months, years, is made up of exchange-units which do not belong to him. Later he will exchange these units (this money-time) for opportunities which will belong to him. This gives him hope, and it breeds the fear that he may not survive the present to make the exchange.

While working he lives only the present of things exterior to him. In this his experience is similar to that of many indigenous workers. The difference is that when the migrant worker clocks-out he does not re-enter his own present.

Nine inches above his pillow he has driven a nail into the wall. On the nail he has hung an alarm clock. From there it wakes him ninety minutes before the shift begins. Around the clock is a votive frescoe of twenty women, nude and shameless. The prayer is that his own virility be one day recognized. The vow is that he will not for an instant forget now what women are like. The pictures have been taken from posters or magazines published in the metropolis. The women are unlike any he has ever spoken to. They have instant breasts, instant cunts, which propose instant sex: the proposition as rapid as the action of the press that printed them.

To make present sacrifices for the sake of the future is an essentially human act: a constituent of the human condition. All stories from all times offer examples. And, in this, his story is as old as the first traveller's. To save money for the sake of one's family's future was a cornerstone of the original capitalist ethic, which prescribed it as the duty of self-help. There are thousands of nineteenth-century moral tales which illustrate the principle.

To make an offering to the future, however, pre-supposes continuity: not necessarily of one's own individual interest (the offering may involve the sacrifice of one's own life), but of the values in which one believes. The sacrifice is offered now in the conviction that it will be recognizable and receivable in the future. The sacrifice, in fact, is to a tradition, whose continuity into the future seems assured. The content of the tradition changes: a religious belief in God's will, the hopes of a family fortune, the destiny of a nation, the necessity of revolution. Yet all are grounded in a sense of continuity, and all seek a confirmation in that.

The migrant worker sacrifices the present for the future under circumstances which continually confound his sense of continuity. Scarcely anything he experiences or witnesses confirms the value of his sacrifice. Only when he returns to redeem his exchange-units of time will he gain acknowledgement for what he has done, or, to be more precise, for the way he has done what he was forced to do. Meanwhile he lives in a situation of almost total unacknowledgement.

True he has at least the company and support of his compatriots who are also migrants. They may live side by side, but they do not live in the same present. They come closest together when they talk about the past. To keep faith with his decision, each man has to picture his own individual future of acknowledgement to himself. And he has to do this countless times every day. Only from this picture can he receive confirmation. To construct the picture he goes back to the past. What is characteristic of the migrant worker is not that he sacrifices the present for the future, but that his condition is such that the value of his present sacrifice is denied. This is why his condition resembles imprisonment.

After work he changes his clothes. Other men's working clothes hang in the same room. They are the clothes of jobs: when discarded, all that remains of the man that worked in them is the smell of sweat. In the clothes room the permanent smell of sweat is a cold smell. Sometimes when he is putting his working clothes on, he shivers: they expect exertion. When he takes them off, there is no acknowledgement.

For the rest of the evening in the barracks he wears something he wore at home – a robe, a coloured shirt, sandals with bare feet, a skull cap, perhaps a woollen shawl. In its folds, or texture, or the way it fits him, there is a residue from the past, and this acts as a kind of physical insulation against the present.

They had eaten but were not yet ready to go to bed. So they sat round the table in the centre of the room which had a single window very high up on one wall. The window had no curtains and it was too high up to look out of. It was hot in the room and the window was open. Through it came the noise of the evening traffic. They worked in the docks cleaning out the holds of ships being refitted. One was complaining about a pain in his shoulder. He complained most nights. Then there was a silence which lasted for nearly ten minutes. The eldest amongst them looked at his watch and announced that it was time for their milk drink. He, the youngest, goes out to prepare it. On the gas stove at the end of the passage, next to the lavatory, he empties the milk into a saucepan. He takes six glasses out of the cold oven of the gas stove. Each glass has a golden emblem of the silhouette of their capital city printed on it. He watches carefully lest the milk boil. Before he pours the milk, he puts a spoon in each glass to prevent it cracking from the heat. Then, with the glasses on a copper-coloured tray, he returns to the room and places one before each man. Meanwhile the elder has placed an embossed silver-coloured sugar bowl in the centre of the table. The bowl is passed round and each man adds two or three spoonfuls of sugar to his milk. They stir their glasses. The youngest smells the milk appreciatively before drinking it. All of them sip the sweet milk slowly. Then they begin to talk. That night the eldest man started to talk about his mother. The others in turn talked about theirs.

The dates, like the telegraph poles, pass.

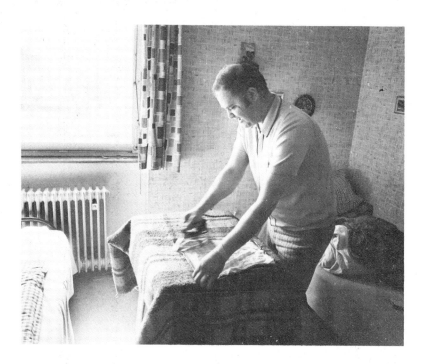

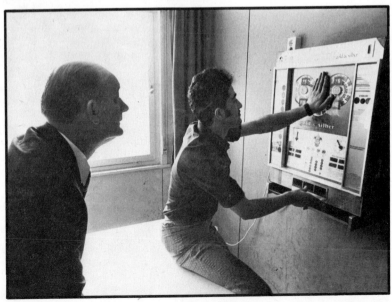

GREEKS IN GREEK CLUB, STUTTGART, GERMANY

GREEKS IN GREEK CLUB, STUTTGART, GERMANY

Time-off cannot be exchanged against anything in the future. It exists in a present which is exterior (like that of work time) but is also meaningless. A pure negation. He tries to avoid it. To fill it with talk about the past. To pretend that it can be measured in exchange-units by thinking of his chores as work time: the pretence fails. To watch the television without following the words. To go to the railway station and wait for the trains to arrive. To play a game because games create their own independent present. To sit thinking of the future. To sing.

Music takes hold of the present, divides it up and builds a bridge with it, which leads to the life's time. The listener and singer borrow the music's intentionality and find in it a lost amalgam of past, present and future. Over the bridge, for as long as the music lasts, he passes backwards and forwards.

When the music stops, the meaninglessness seeps back. To find the present meaningless is to feel oneself dead and con-demned.

But after work and on Sundays it is hellish.

Other facts are relevant. That he is barred from natural communication by a language barrier. That his rejection by the indigenous population as a natural inferior denies his present being, and peremptorily throws him again and again back into the past. That his living conditions are humiliating. That he is sexually deprived.

But I believe the full measure of the violence being done to him is revealed by what happens within him.

What has happened within him is not distinct from what happens within millions of others who are not migrant workers. It is simply more extreme. He experiences suddenly as an individual, as a man who believes he is choosing his own life, what the industrial consumer societies have experienced gradually through generations without the effort of choosing. He lives the content of our institutions: they transform him violently. They do not need to transform us. We are already within them.

One morning after working the night shift he looks up at a street corner. Few citizens are yet about. The buses are still running fast: the traffic of the day has not yet slowed them down. In places the roads are wet from having been washed. Is he walking back to his bed. Is he cleaning the street. Is he clocking-in for the day shift. He looks up and on the corner of a roof, four stories high, he sees the silhouette of a large bird: a bird that would have to be held in the arms, not just in the hand. A second one appears from behind a chimney-stack.

They are duck who have flown from the river across the rail-yards and alighted on the roof at the corner, above the neon capital letters: **OMEGA**. The sight of these large birds at roof level, alighted, brings sudden pleasure to him: it was a sight he never expected to see in the city. The pleasure compresses, reduces in his mind the months before his annual return to the village. For a moment in the early morning, when the buses still run fast, the four months of a hundred and twenty days seem like two months of only sixty days.

TOURISTS VISITING SOUNION, GREECE

CHILDREN PLAYING SKITTLES, TRAPETTO, SICILY

His solitude is like iron in the rain
his palms are red with rust
on the foreign side of the river
with the dead
in the dark
(on the wire of his bunk)
he whistles for the ferry.

Whistles to cross as conqueror
like
Suleiman the lawgiver
Albuquerque who died on the way
or the great Alexander*

and to hear at last others talk
of the traveller's homecoming.

---

* Each of these was a type of conquistador. Five out of the six European
countries from which migrant workers come have in the past been pow
who conquered and colonized.

A Yugoslav: To go home? Of course. As soon as I can. You can see I live out of a suitcase. I buy nothing. What should I do with the things I bought? You can't cart them around from lodging to lodging. It would be different if I was going to stay here, if we were going to settle. But I could never do that. I'd always choose the life at home in my own country. One day it will be better at home than abroad and, when I go back there, I'll be able to work for myself and I'll build myself a house. It'll be a kind of paradise. If only the wages at home were a bit higher and if everyone could find work there, nobody would leave to go abroad.

YOUGOSLAVIE

TRAIN AND CATTLE MARKET, SERBIA, YUGOSLAVIA

Most legal migrants are able to return home for about a month every year. The timing of their release usually depends upon the convenience of production. For example most French factories close down during August and so the migrant workers go home. In Switzerland and Germany building and construction work becomes difficult or impossible during the two coldest winter months, and so it is then that the migrant workers are dismissed – with pay for one month only.

Special trains are put on and special flights. Some drive the thousands of kilometres in the cars they have bought. They drive fast for they are in a hurry. Doubly so. Their release is limited to so many days; and by now their physical impatience to be back is as irresistible as a tide coming in. They drive all night taking turns at the wheel. The others doze, cheeks pressed against the plastic seats.

A few go home slowly, saving money on the journey. Their time is unlimited, because they have sworn that when they return, they will do anything legal or illegal – rather than depart a second time.

He has a fiancée. He is married. He has no children. He has six children. During his absence his wife bore his first child.

Only if he becomes a trouble-maker does he earn an identity; and then he will be recognized in order to be kept out.

Letters during the year have been hard to write and his mother has spoken to his younger brother, who has written the words. He has presents for them all. Carefully chosen small presents, for he eschews extravagance. The building of the house comes before everything; when it is finished, he will come home to live in it for good.

There is an approximate tariff: it takes five years' work abroad to help support the family and save enough to buy the materials for building a house. The building the family do themselves. It takes three years to buy a car or tractor or the tools necessary for most artisanal trades.

There is another tariff of bribes: for a job in a government office, for exemption from conscription, for a commercial licence, for getting a brother out of trouble with the police. Each bribe can now be translated into months or years of factory-time.

For weeks he has plotted how to smuggle three watches through. Customs officials discriminate against migrant workers in accordance with the international convention that: **WHEN THE POOR HAVE MONEY IT POINTS TO A CRIME.** It will be the last contest of the year and he believes he has won it already. When he boarded the train, with his suitcase and packages, all that had been taken away from him was returned to him: independence, manhood, private address, voice, proclivity to love, right to age. Nobody handed these things over to him like the confiscated contents of his pockets, but they were returned to him by his destination.

Kilometres and hours stream past the train window. They fill the wells of his mind. For once, what is happening to him whilst he sleeps, confirms his wishes.

When he shaves in the train corridor he looks at the face in the mirror critically; for months the face has only looked at him slyly, with complicity. He is returning to himself at last acknowledged. What he has had to hide for eleven months will now be evident to everyone who sees him: that he is not inferior but superior.

HOUSEHOLD GOODS BOUGHT BY TURKISH MIGRANT, ANATOLIA, TURKEY

RETURNED TURKISH MIGRANT WITH HIS CAR

He gets off the train in the capital of his province. When he left, its new unfamiliar sights impressed him. Now he looks at it with a kind of familiar astonishment. He knows all the words he hears. If a passer-by, a stranger, stopped him and said: You should be ashamed of yourself! his first reaction would be of delight at being addressed by a stranger in his own language. The glances he receives, however, suggest a very different greeting. Nobody in the large square outside the station knows his name, but everybody knows where he has come from, and their glances, far from speaking of shame, are admiring and envious.

He has changed faster than his country. The economic conditions which formed his decision to leave have not improved; they may have deteriorated.

Of the countries from which migrants come, Yugoslavia is the exception in that it has by far the highest economic growth rate. In the period 1945–65 it was the highest in the world. Yet if the Yugoslav Croats now working abroad were willing to work at home for only half as much as they earn at present, this would still be half as much again as the average wage in Croatia. More important still, the jobs, irrespective of the wages paid, do not exist. It is foreseen that in the next few years there will only be enough jobs for a third of those now abroad who wish to return.

In Turkey unemployment is increasing. In 1963 more than half of a sample of Turkish migrants, questioned while abroad, believed that on their return they would find work easily. Three years later only 13 per cent believed it would be easy. Today there would be fewer still.

In Portugal the average income is $350 a year. The population is eight and a half million, and there are estimated to be 1.6 million Portuguese working abroad.

According to his calculations, his annual return is a preparation for his final return. None of his experience has ever led him to doubt the power of money in hand. He is nearer to fulfilling his plan.

To be one's own master in the economic as well as the social sense.
To receive all the money which the finished job brings in.
To have a shop.
To run a taxi service.
To start a garage.
To buy better land and cultivate it. To buy a tractor.
To become an independent mason.

Sometimes:
To become a tailor.
To work in an office.
To mend radios.
To buy land and rent it to somebody else to work.
To start a photography business.
To sell goods from the city.

These are his plans for the final return. He does not plan to continue working in a factory. (Nor do the factory jobs exist.)

Near the bus station he finds a car, driven by two compatriots who have come from Zurich. They are going near his village. A beggar asks for money. He gives it.

As they drive off, they light up cigarettes with their lighters from the city. They pass the sentinel of the first animal. Pass Friend.

Along the road are carts and boys holding out small pears to sell.

Sitting back in the car, manufactured in the metropolis where he works, he has become the latest rumour of the city. He is wearing its clothes. He has its shoes on his feet. He has three of its watches keeping perfect time.

The trees are in their place.

From within the rumour, its window rolled down, he watches his village approach. To here, for eleven months, he has sent its money.

His mother frail and tiny in his arms.

For a whole month now the photographs will become redundant.

His uncle, who is still alive, looks at him with a different look. It is hard to know whether this look is out of respect for the honour he has acquired or because his uncle has come closer to death.

For the first time for a year he is recognized as desirable. For the first time for a year he can afford to be gentle. For the first time for a year he can choose to be silent.

They talk of his final return.

The final return is mythic. It gives meaning to what might otherwise be meaningless. It is larger than life. It is the stuff of longing and prayers. But it is also mythic in the sense that, as imagined, it never happens. There is no final return.

Because the village has scarcely changed since he left, there is still no livelihood there for him. When he carries out one of his plans, he will become the victim of the same economic stagnation which first forced him to leave.

He will join the already swollen and parasitic service sector. The economy of the village or the nearest town is incapable of supporting him. Two or three years after his final return he or other members of his family will be compelled to go abroad once more.

Unchanging as the village is, he will never again see it as he did before he left. He is seen differently and he sees differently.

His prestige as a returned and successful migrant is considerable. (Given this prestige, it would be unseemly for him to take on a menial local job.) The villagers now respect him as a man of different experience. He has seen and received and achieved things which they have not. He is the interpreter, the transmitter, the conveyer of these things to them; the things range from money through commodities to information. They seize upon them to put them to their own use. Gradually he is stripped of what he came back with. Not because his family or the friends of his family are ruthless, but because nothing else is possible. Neither he nor they, whilst remaining in the village, can re-produce any of the things he brought back. His different experience is not applicable to the village as it is. It belongs elsewhere. The village can only use what the time-units of his experience can be exchanged for. He has become a wage earner. They have become the dependants of his wage. Yet he must always accept their judgement. And they cannot allow for his experience of the metropolis. If they knew of them, they would call his deprivations there shameful. The village behaves like a beggared king. If he questions its judgement too openly, not even his newly-won prestige will save him from being condemned as an agitator.

An assured place for him no longer exists in his village.

Such an end can be subsumed under several generalizing categories in order to render it normal: The Road to Development: The Unification of Europe: The History of Capitalism: even The Oncoming Revolutionary Struggle. But the categories do not make him less homeless. In space and time.

TURKISH CARPET-SELLER IN GERMANY. A NUMBER OF MIGRANTS COME
PRIVATELY TO SELL GOODS TO THEIR FELLOW COUNTRYMEN. HE IS SELLING

„10 Prozent aller Auto fahrenden höheren Beamten würden eine Anhalterin in Hot Pants mitnehmen."

Auch diese Aussage beruht auf Ergebnissen der SPIEGEL-Marktforschung.

Wer Entscheidungen trifft im Marketing, in Verkauf oder Werbung, sollte die Untersuchungen des SPIEGEL-Verlags kennen. Sie liefern Daten und Informationen über Verbrauchs-, Gebrauchs- und Investitionsgüter ebenso wie über Dienstleistungen. SPIEGEL-Untersuchungen sind Planungshilfen.

deren Informationsgehalt in der Branche anerkannt ist.

Umfassende Markt- und Mediadaten, die nach statistisch-mathematisch anerkannten Verfahren aufbereitet worden sind, können Entscheidungen erleichtern. Wenn Marketingprobleme zu lösen sind, ist individuelle Beratung notwendig. Das Team vom Marketing Research* verspricht:

„Der Service des SPIEGEL-Verlags steht allen Unternehmen zur Verfügung. Auch Ihnen."

Rufen Sie an oder ben Sie.

DER SPIEGEL

Is it very large, the city? his younger cousin asks him.

It is very large, and to reach it takes three days and
nights.

We still go and watch the train from the river, the
train you said went to Paris, it passes every evening when we are
swimming there. We wave and the ones at the windows sometimes
wave back. Did you come by that train?

Yes, but it does not stop here.

It often stops on the bend.

Not always.

You could jump down.

And supposing it did not stop and the signals were not red? You have much to learn, boy cousin. There are papers which tell where the trains stop and at what time. At the station in F— there are more than a hundred rails which come together, they cover ground wider than the space between the cemetery and the tower.

Does everybody have a car?

The cars are so close together in the street that it's like a river. A river of many colours. The cars are the colours of all the fruits in the world.

What colour will be the one you buy?

The colour is not important. What matters is how long the engine lasts.

Do they drive fast?

Not as fast as us. You know how we say of a man that he comes back before he goes? Well, they are like that in their cars. They go in circles, round and round. You see the same person in the same car in almost the same place four times in the same day. They have nowhere to go.

If I left like you?

How strong are you?

Look at me.

Not only in your arms and back. Here too.

In the neck, yes.

In the bottom of your stomach?

Like an ox.

In the brain and your balls. You have to be strong for your son too.

I haven't a wife yet.

You plan for your son before he is born.

I am strong there too.

They have tests to prove how strong you are. Several doctors look at you every way. If you pass their tests, you can say you are really strong. Just as if your uncle buys a ram, it will not be a sick one.

There aren't people ill there?

Very few amongst us. They have hospitals as large as the railyards. And you don't shit against the walls in their hospitals.

How would I find work there?

For the strong there are always jobs. There is no need ever to stop working, there is so much work.

When you come in from work, who has cooked the food?

There are women who do that. They serve us. There is a television where we eat too.

You watch the football?

You could watch every match. But it is better to work at night because the night pays even more than the day.

The stars more than the sun.

The lighting there makes the night like day, but the night pays more.

People say women there are not like ours.

You will not at first believe your eyes. But I believe mine now. Their women have no patience. They do not know how to dress. And they eat all the time in front of you. If you don't want to be eaten, you'd better have your wits about you. (Laughs.)

Do they? (he makes a sign with his hands using four fingers.)

In airplanes as well.

The same?

All over the world it is the same and different.

When did you buy this? (the young man touches his cousin's sleeve.) It honours you, cousin. Anybody seeing you wearing this will say: this is a man who has come back from the abroad with what he went to find. How much do you earn there?

It is too soon to tell you that. But I will tell you that I earn more than the tax collector.

Let me go back with you when you go.

It cannot be decided between you and me.

All the family will agree with whatever you say, now that you have come back. You have only to say the word. Tell them I should come. Tell them.

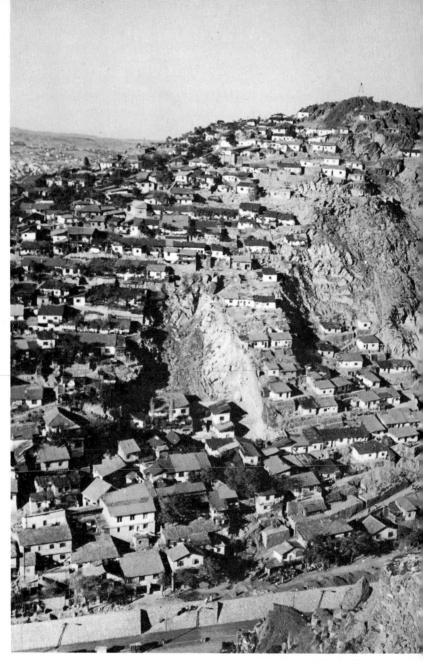

VILLAGERS FROM ANATOLIA COME TO ANKARA. ON THE CITY OUTSKIRTS THEY
BUILD SHACKS TO LIVE IN. THE ROOF MUST BE PUT UP DURING THE FIRST NIGHT
OF BUILDING. IF BY MORNING THERE IS A ROOF, THE CITY AUTHORITIES DO NOT
HAVE THE RIGHT TO DESTROY THE SHACK. THE SHACKS ARE WITHOUT SANITA-
TION OR WATER. FOR MANY THIS IS THE FIRST STEP TOWARDS EMIGRATION

To be homeless is to be nameless. He. The existence of a migrant worker.

Organizations

The following is a short list of organizations created out of the life and struggle of immigrant workers.

Britain

Transport and General Workers Union, Industrial Workers Branch
    21 Theobalds Road, London WC1
Association of Turkish Progressives
    56 Mansfield Road, Ilford, Essex
Spanish Club Antonio Machado
    236 Westbourne Park Road, London W11
Portuguese League
    18 Fleet Road, London NW3
Indian Workers Association of Great Britain
    13 Nanson Road, Coldean, Brighton, Sussex
Standing Conference of Pakistani Organizations
    57 Delahayes Road, Hale, Altrincham, Cheshire
Federation of Bangladesh Organizations
    66 Fargate, Sheffield, Yorkshire

France

G.I.S.T.I. (Groupe d'Information et de Soutien des Travailleurs Immigrés)
    15 rue Guy-Lussac, 75005 Paris
F.A.S.T.I. (Fédération des Associations de Solidarité avec les Travailleurs Immigrés)
    103 rue Réaumur, 75002 Paris
C.I.M.A.D.E. (Service Œcuménique d'Entraide)
    176 rue de Grenelle, 75007 Paris
M.R.A.P. (Mouvement contre le Racisme, l'Antisémitisme et pour la Paix)
    120 rue de Saint-Denis, 75002 Paris

Switzerland

Association de Travailleurs Emigrés en Suisse (A.T.E.E.S.)
    Foyer Cerventes, 9A rue Contamines, CN 1206, Genève
Centres de Contact (entre immigrés et Suisses)
    C.P.20, CH 8053, Zurich
    rue Saint-Laurent 2, CH 1003, Lausanne

Marktgasse 50, CH 3000, Berne
>Fronwagplatz 25, CH Schaffhouse
Fédération des Colonies Libres Italiennes
>Lagerstr. 107, CH 8004, Zurich
Commission Sociale Romande
>rue Georgette 8, CH 1003, Lausanne
Commission Protestante Suisse-Allemanique pour
les Travailleurs Étrangers
>Hirschengraben 40, CH 8001, Zurich
Communauté de Travail Catholique pour les Travailleurs Étrangers
>Löwenstr. 3, CH 6000, Lucerne

Holland

Werkgroep Communicatie Gastarbeiders
>Postbus 167, Venlo
Werkgroep Buitenlandse Arbeiders
>Doeslaan 12, Leiderdorp
Aktie Komité Pro-Gastarbeider
>Jacobusstraat 45A, Rotterdam
Werkgroep Dar-bak
>Prins Hendriklaan 21, Amsterdam
Werkgroep Migranten
>Sjef Teunis, Plompetorengracht 10, Utrecht

Germany

Verein der Arbeiter und Studenten aus der Türkei
>(Bielefeld und Umgebung) 48 Bielefeld, Siechenmarschstr. 16
Verein der Arbeiter und Studenten aus der Türkei
>(Bochum und Umgebung) Celal Bicici, 463 Bochum, Marktstr. 118 Zimmer 123
Türkische Arbeiter Verein im Dortmund
>46 Dortmund, Blücherstr. 27
Kultür Bund im München
>(Türkiye Kültür Birliği) 8 munchen 2, Gabelsbergerstr. 65
Der Revolutionär (Devrimci) Türkische Zeitung
>Devrimci 5 Koln 1, Postfach 25 03 46

List of Illustrations

Acknowledgements

In this book there were quotations unacknowledged on the pages on which they occurred. This was not out of disrespect for the writers or books from which the quotations were taken. On the contrary. It was because, at those moments, the quotations hopefully acquired a universality; and to have insisted upon authorship would have been to divert attention from a larger truth. The quotations were as follows:

Page
11   'The Seventh', poem by Attila József, translated by John Batki, London, Carcanet Press Publications, p.68.

21   'In current descriptions of the world . . . the great majority of its people.' Raymond Williams, 'The Country and the City', London, Chatto & Windus, p.279.

21   'Every Sunday . . . up to heaven.' Quoted in 'The Pueblo' by Ronald Fraser, London, Allen Lane, p.44.

35   'Although monopoly capital succeeds . . . in the twentieth century.' Ernest Mandel, 'The laws of uneven develop- ment', London, 'New Left Review' No.59, p.22.

36   'In most underdeveloped countries . . . upheavals at home.' Paul Baran, 'The Political Economy of Growth', Harmonds- worth, Penguin Books, p.316.

38   Portuguese migrant quoted by Juliette Minces, 'Les Travailleurs Etrangers en France', Paris, Editions du Seuil, p.70.

40   'Like all the swollen capitals . . . a primitive character.' Constantine Tsoucalas, 'The Greek Tragedy', Harmondsworth, Penguin Books, p.127.

43   Turkish migrant, quoted by Juliette Minces, op cit., p.81.

67   'Trams passed one another . . . piled-up bricks, stones.' James Joyce, 'Ulysses', Harmondsworth, Penguin Books, p.164.

Page

68   'Migration involves . . . other factors of production.' Stephen Castles and Godula Kosack, 'Immigrant Workers and Class Structure in Western Europe', London, Oxford University Press, p.409.

94   Henry Ford, quoted by Huw Beynon, 'Working for Ford', Harmondsworth, Penguin Books, p.116.

99   British worker at Fords, quoted by Huw Beynon, op cit., p.114.

104   Marx, 'Capital', vol.1, London, Lawrence & Wishart, p.898.

104   Marx, op. cit., p.401.

105   Henry Ford, quoted by Huw Beynon, op. cit., p.108.

126   'There are a number of reasons for immigrant workers' high accident rate . . . reduces attentiveness.' Castles and Kosack, op. cit., p.340.

135   'No matter how limited . . . the other end of the world.' Yashar Kemal, 'Memed My Hawk', London, Collins, p.76.

176   Italian migrant, quoted by Castles and Kosack, op. cit., p.356.

Many people helped in the making of this book.

Among them: Victor Anant, Max Arian, Anthony Barnett, George Catephores, Colin Chambers, Howard Daniel, Chris Fox, Roger Hart, Beverly Hiro, Dilip Hiro, Chantal Scheidecker, Nel Soetens, Nikos Stangos, Jaka Štulav, Manuel Torres, Jerney Vilfan, Joža Vilfan, Maria Vilfan, and a librarian in the Stockholm Public Library.